Martin C

PLAYS THREE

Martin Crimp was born in 1956. His play *Attempts on
Her Life* (1997) established his international reputation.
His other work for theatre includes *The Rest Will Be
Familiar to You from Cinema*, *In the Republic of
Happiness*, *Play House*, *The City*, *Fewer Emergencies*,
Cruel and Tender, *The Country*, *The Treatment*, *Getting
Attention*, *No One Sees the Video*, *Play with Repeats*,
Dealing with Clair and *Definitely the Bahamas*. He is
also the author of two texts, *Into the Little Hill* and
Written on Skin, for operas by George Benjamin. His
many translations of French plays include works by
Genet, Ionesco, Koltès, Marivaux and Molière.

MARTIN CRIMP

Plays Three

Cruel and Tender
Fewer Emergencies
The City
Play House
Definitely the Bahamas
In the Republic of Happiness

Introduced by the author

FABER & FABER

This collection first published in 2015
by Faber and Faber Ltd
74–77 Great Russell Street
London WC1B 3DA

Typeset by Country Setting, Kingsdown, Kent CT14 8ES
Printed in England by CPI Group (UK) Ltd, Croydon CR0 4YY

A CIP record for this book is available from the British Library

978-0-571-32536-8

2 4 6 8 10 9 7 5 3 1

Contents

Contents

The Writer on Holiday

It's the 1950s — the decade I was born — and Roland
Barthes pictures the Writer on Holiday with the
maximum affection and contempt. The Writer is in his
blue pyjamas — travelling — forgive me — I don't have
the book in front of me — but travelling, I believe, along
the Nile or is it the Congo river — dressed in his blue
pyjamas but still writing — since the Writer, says Barthes,
is unable not to write — every moment, says Barthes,
for the Writer is a moment of writing — writing can't
stop — even on holiday, says Barthes, the Writer, dressed
in his blue pyjamas, or wearing his holiday hat, will
write and write, will correct proofs, will imagine new
forms for fiction and invent new kinds of theatre that
the theatre world is so evidently agog for. How slyly —
claims Barthes — has the Writer with the collusion of
the bourgeois press adopted this relatively new-made
proletarian institution, *the holiday*, and turned it to his
advantage. Watch him toss his tanning lotion and
ridiculous shorts into his holiday holdall just like the rest
of us! See how even the author of *The Phenomenology
of the Ego* staggers out of the freezing Atlantic like an
ordinary human being and offers to the camera the same
brave human grin and — emerging from the kind of
trunks the French call *cock-squeezers* — his slightly
disappointing thighs. But this — claims Roland Barthes
back in the 1950s — is the trick of it. Since the Writer
allows himself — and yes it's always a man — allows
himself to appear ordinary — to like pretty girls and —
if I'm remembering Barthes correctly — certain kinds of
cheese — only to prove to the world how *extra*-ordinary

vii

he is, given he combines his taste for cheese et cetera, girls and so on, with non-stop literary production. Barthes invokes — at least I think this is true — I need to check — but I think he goes on to invoke the lives of saints, whose banal human origins serve to set off their amazing deaths and miracles like jewels. The Writer — concludes Barthes — is in fact saying: *The fact that I rent for some weeks of the summer a small cottage by the sea and can be glimpsed through the hibiscus sitting outside at the breakfast table barefoot wearing blue pyjamas and drinking perfectly ordinary coffee out of a cracked rented cup EVEN AS I GO ON WRITING is none other than proof of my divinity.*

And yes it's true — I do feel pretty divine this morning — yes I do feel a bit like god — a little ashamed, as I look back over them, of some of the things I've made — but often proud — less interested than I used to be in girls and cheese — but still looking forward to my holidays.

MC, June 2015

CRUEL AND TENDER

after
Sophocles' *Trachiniae*

Cruel and Tender was commissioned by the Wiener Festwochen, the Chichester Festival Theatre and the Young Vic Theatre Company. It was first presented, in a co-production with the Théâtre des Bouffes du Nord and Ruhrfestspiele Recklinghausen, at the Young Vic, London, on 5 May 2004. The cast was as follows:

Laela Georgina Ackerman
Nicola Jessica Claire
The General Joe Dixon
Cathy Lourdes Faberes
James Toby Fisher
Amelia Kerry Fox
Jonathan Michael Gould
Iolaos Aleksandar Mikic
Rachel Nicola Redmond
Richard David Sibley
A Boy Stuart Brown / Mario Vieira

Direction Luc Bondy
Set Richard Peduzzi
Costumes Rudy Sabounghi
Lighting Dominique Bruguière
Sound Paul Arditti
Wigs and make-up Cécile Kretschmar
Dramaturg Geoffrey Layton
Executive Producer Nicky Pallot
Casting Director Sam Jones
Assistant Director Lucy Jameson

Luc Bondy, fascinated by Sophocles' rarely performed tragedy, encouraged Martin Crimp to produce a new piece taking the original subject in a new direction for his first English-language production.

Characters

Amelia, forties
The General, forties, her husband
James, late teens, their son
Richard, fifties, a journalist
Jonathan, thirties, a government minister

Amelia's three helpers

Housekeeper (Rachel)
Physiotherapist (Cathy)
Beautician (Nicola)

Two children from sub-Saharan Africa

Laela, eighteen
Edu, a boy, about six

Iolaos, a friend of the General

Note on the Text

A slash like this / indicates the point of interruption
in overlapping dialogue.

The time is the present.
The place is the General and Amelia's
temporary home close to an international airport.

Part One

ONE

Amelia holds a white pillow. Her Housekeeper tidies the room.

Amelia
> There are women who believe
> all men are rapists.
> I don't believe that
> because if I did believe that
> how—as a woman—could I go on living
> with the label 'victim'?
> Because I am not a victim—oh no—
> that's not a part I'm willing to play—believe me.

She smiles.

> I was just fifteen
> living with my father
> living very very quietly with my father
> when the first man came to my father
> wanting me. He described to him
> the various ways he wanted me
> while I listened outside the door in the very short skirt
> and the very high-heeled agonising shoes
> I had begged and begged to be allowed to wear.
> I ran up to my room. Locked the door. Stopped eating.

She smiles.

> Three years later and I'm married—
> incredibly—to a soldier—
> to the only man
> who has ever remembered the colour of my eyes

after a single conversation under a tree.
I am eighteen years old and I have a house
a husband and a bed—
a bed with white pillows—
and a child.
I abandon my course at university
to become the mother of a child—
even if he—the father—
the soldier who is by now of course the great general—
only sees this child at distant intervals
like a farmer inspecting a crop
in a remote field.
Because my husband is sent out
on one operation after another
with the aim—the apparent aim—
of eradicating terror: not understanding
that the more he fights terror
the more he creates terror—
and even invites terror—who has no eyelids—
into his own bed.
And now those operations are over
instead of being respected for having risked his life
time and time and time again
he is accused of war crimes—murdering a civilian.
They say he dragged this boy off a bus
and cut his heart out in front of the crowd.
Which is why we were shipped out here
to the suburbs
close to the airport perimeter
and told 'Don't talk to the press' blah blah blah
while my husband vanishes—
is driven away in a black car
with black glass in the windows
and I'm told nothing—
nothing now for over a year.
Are you saying that's reasonable?

Housekeeper I'm not saying anything, Amelia: that's not my job. My job is to run the house—clean it—make sure the ironing's done and that the fridge gets regularly defrosted. Because I'm not here—I'm sorry, Amelia, but I'm not here to offer advice. Although if that *was* my job . . .

Amelia Oh?

Housekeeper Yes—if that *was* my job, I'd like to ask why you don't get that son of yours to do something— why can't James—why can't James find out where his father is?—he's old enough.

Amelia (*calls*) James.

Housekeeper Most boys his age are / working.

Amelia (*calls*) James. Come here.

Housekeeper Or studying. I mean what's wrong with him earning some / *money*?

Amelia (*calls*) James. I want you.

James appears, reluctantly. Pause.

James What is it, Mum? I'm busy.

Housekeeper Don't you dare talk to your mother / like that.

Amelia (*smiles*) Keep out of it, please. (*Slight pause.*) James?

James Yes?

Amelia Look at me when I talk to you. (*Slight pause.*) I SAID WILL YOU PLEASE LOOK AT ME.

He looks at her.

I want you to find out where your father is. (*Slight pause.*) I said: I want you to find out where your / father is.

James I know where my father is.

Amelia Oh? Where?

James (*imitating her*) 'Oh? Where?'

Housekeeper Don't talk to your / mother like that.

Amelia Keep out of it.

James He's in Gisenyi.

Amelia He's what?

James He's in a war-zone, Mum. He was supposed to be in Asia but they're saying he's now in Africa. They're saying he's been sent to Africa and is attacking or is about to attack the camp or the city or the whatever it's supposed to be of Gisenyi. (*Grins.*) Don't you read the papers? (*Pause.*) What's wrong?

Amelia See if it's true.

James What d'you mean, Mum, see if it's true?

Amelia Go there. See if it's true.

James Go there? It's a war-zone.

Housekeeper Do what you're told.

Amelia That's right—she's right—don't answer me back, James—just do what you're told.

   Slight pause.

James Mum?

Housekeeper I'll help him pack.

James Mum?

Amelia And he'll need a visa. What? What? Don't you love your father?

Housekeeper Don't you love your parents, James?

Amelia suddenly laughs and throws the pillow at James, who catches it.

James What's this for?

Amelia So you can sleep on the plane, sweetheart.

TWO

Amelia has cotton-wool between her toes. Her Beautician paints her toenails, while her Physiotherapist massages or manipulates her shoulders. Amelia is reading documents.

Physiotherapist How are you, Amelia? How're you feeling?

Beautician Says she's not sleeping.

Physiotherapist Oh? Not sleeping? Why's that?

Beautician Says she feels old.

Physiotherapist Well, she doesn't look old.

Beautician I keep telling her that.

Physiotherapist Tense though.

Beautician Mmm?

Physiotherapist Tense—very tense—very tense in the shoulders—very tense in the neck. Aren't you, Amelia.

Beautician She's not listening.

Physiotherapist She needs to relax more.

Pause.

What about exercise?

Beautician She doesn't go out.

Physiotherapist I meant the machine: aren't you using your machine?

Beautician She hates that machine.

Physiotherapist It's a good machine: it's one of the best there is. If you don't use your machine, Amelia, how d'you expect to sleep?

Beautician You mean she's not fit?

Physiotherapist I mean she's not tired: she's fit, but she's / not tired.

Beautician She's always tired: she never sleeps.

Physiotherapist Exactly my point.

Pause.

Well that's exactly the point I'm trying / to make.

Beautician She waits for the light.

Physiotherapist She ought to jog, she ought to be out there running, she ought to be taking more / exercise.

Beautician She waits for the light. She says she just lies there waiting for the light. She's depressed: she misses her / husband.

Physiotherapist Because I refuse to believe this is psychological.

Beautician Don't move, Amelia: it's still wet.

Pause. They move away and lower their voices.

Of course it's psychological: she's like a bird in a box— look at her.

Physiotherapist Like a what?

Beautician A bird—a bird in a box.

Physiotherapist You mean like a parrot?

Beautician I mean like a bird—like a wounded bird. Not like a parrot—like a bird / in a box.

Amelia
Please. Stop now. Don't try and sympathise.
You're not married
and you don't have children.
When you do have children
they'll break into your life
you'll see
like tiny tiny terrorists
who refuse to negotiate.
And when you have husbands
by which I mean men—
not these boys
not these boys who collect you on your nights off
and drive you in shirts ironed by their mothers
to the nearest multiplex
or back to their one-room flats that look out over
the lined-up trolleys in the supermarket car park
for the inept sex they've read about in magazines—
but men—hurt men—
men whose minds are blank
who fuck you the way they fuck the enemy—
I mean with the same tenderness—
when you understand that
then I will accept your sympathy.
(*Laughs.*) I'm sorry: I'm being cruel.
I'm very very pleased—yes—with my toenails:
   thank you
and if I've failed to use my exercise machine
'one of the best there is'—really?—
then I apologise.

Only these papers . . .
these papers are worrying me:
I found them in a drawer—
he's been—d'you see—look—last year—to a solicitor
and in case of his quote death
or mental incapacity unquote
gives power of attorney over his estate
'and over all things leased or assigned thereunto'
to James.
Which is odd not only because death
is not something he ever seriously considered
but also because—yes? what is it?

Housekeeper has appeared.

Housekeeper Someone to see you.

Amelia Well show them in. Because the fact is—
no—stop—wait—who?

Housekeeper A man with flowers.

Amelia
Flowers—good—show him in. But also odd because—
unless I'm not reading it properly—
and I obviously can't be reading it properly—
because the whole thing
this whole ridiculous document seems to be written
as if I no longer exist. (*Smiles.*)

*Housekeeper has reappeared with Richard, a man in
his fifties with a greying beard, holding a bouquet of
flowers.*

Richard Amelia?

Amelia Yes?

Richard Forgive me barging in like this but I have
fantastic news. I was just at the press-conference and,

although details still have to be confirmed, what's clear is
that the General has won some kind of decisive victory.
(*Slight pause.*) They're saying it's a turning point.

Amelia I'm sorry? What 'press-conference'? What
'victory'? Who are you? Why did you let this man / into
my house?

Richard I'm your friend, Amelia.

Amelia I don't have any friends with beards.

Richard My name is Richard. You once very kindly
allowed me to interview you. We had lunch in a hotel.

Amelia Richard. Of course you are.

She smiles, kisses his cheek, takes the flowers.

What gorgeous flowers. (*to Housekeeper*) Put these in
water / would you.

Richard The minister's still taking questions so I thought
I'd get here first and bring you the good news. Any chance
of a drink?

Amelia But why isn't he here?

Richard I've told you: he's taking questions. You know
what journalists are like—probe probe probe—why do
we always assume we're being / lied to?

Amelia My husband.

Richard I'm sorry?

Amelia Why isn't my *husband* here?

Richard Well he has to . . . secure the city, Amelia.
There's very little—what's the word—infrastructure.
(*Pause.*) Aren't you pleased?

Amelia Mmm?

Richard He's alive. Aren't you happy?

Amelia I'm very very happy. Thank you.

Richard Please don't cry. I wouldn't've come if I'd known this would / upset you.

Amelia I'm very very happy. And I'm very pleased you've come. Forgive me for crying.

She puts her arms round him and clings. He's embarrassed—doesn't know how to react.

Dance with me.

Richard I'm sorry?

Amelia Please. It's so long since I've danced.

Music: 1938 recording of Billie Holiday singing 'My Man'. They dance.

Voice of Billie Holiday
Sometimes I say
if I could just get away
with my man.
He goes straight
sure as fate
for it never is too late
for a man.

I just like to dream
of a cottage by a stream
with my man
where a few flowers grew
and perhaps a kid or two
like my man.

And then my eyes get wet I 'most forget
till he gets hot and tells me not to talk such rot.

16

Oh my man I love him so
he'll never know.
All my life is just despair
but I don't care.
When he takes me in his arms
the world is bright all right.

What's the difference if I say I'll go away
when I know I'll come back on my knees some day.

For whatever my man is
I'm his for ever more.

*As they continue to dance, the Housekeeper brings in
Jonathan—the minister—and with him two children
from sub-Saharan Africa: a girl of about eighteen and
a boy of about six.*

*Jonathan watches, then whispers to Housekeeper, who
turns off the music.*

Amelia Jonathan! How are you? How nice to *see* you!
(*Laughs.*) Who are these children?

Jonathan You seem very happy.

Amelia I *am* very happy—assuming it's true.

Jonathan Assuming what's true?

Amelia Well, the news of course. *Is* it true?

Jonathan Yes.

Amelia He's alive.

Jonathan Yes.

Amelia And unhurt?

Jonathan Yes.

Amelia I'm so relieved.

Jonathan Yes.

In the background Richard opens champagne and begins to fill glasses.

Well, yes, Amelia, I think we / *all* are.

Amelia (*laughs*) But who are these children? Are they *yours*?

Jonathan Do they look like my children?

Amelia Why did he bring his children? Have you been arguing with / your *wife*?

Jonathan These are not my children, Amelia. These are survivors.

Amelia Oh? (*Laughs.*) Survivors of what?

Richard (*raising glass*) Cheers.

Amelia Survivors of what?

Jonathan The only—in fact—apparently—survivors of your husband's assault. (*to Richard*) Cheers.

Amelia So why have you brought them to my house? I don't understand. Where is my husband? I want to see him.

Jonathan To see him? Well, listen, Amelia, it's a war—and—strictly off the record—while we are—and absolutely correctly are—claiming a military success—which—in military terms—don't misunderstand me—it most certainly is. Nevertheless the international community—as is its right—needs reassurance—it needs to be reassured that the General's actions were justified. And I'm happy to say that your husband—with the full backing I can assure you of this government—is putting up a robust and detailed defence.

The child-soldier thing has made our lives particularly difficult—since nobody likes killing children—whereas children themselves seem to find death and dismemberment one big joke. And of course the bus incident did your husband huge damage—although—in our opinion—the so-called child—terrorist, we would prefer to say—posed an immediate threat to our security to which the General responded in his own inimitable way.

Don't get me wrong, Amelia: we're thrilled—we're truly thrilled about what's happened. Because over the last year the General tracked that child back—he tracked that child back to the child's father. And what he discovered was that the father—a man called—yes?

Richard Seratawa.

Jonathan A man called—exactly—thank you—Seratawa—that Seratawa was using the camp—well not camp but city—was using the city of Gisenyi—is this right?— to recruit and to train terrorists—many of them, I'm sorry to say, children.

So what do you do? I'll tell you what you do, Amelia, you send in the General. You tell him to forget blue cards. You tell him to forget the conventional rules of engagement. Because if you want to root out terror—and I believe we all of us want to root out terror—there is only one rule: kill. We wanted that city pulverised—and I mean literally pulverised—the shops, the schools, the hospitals, the libraries, the bakeries, networks of fountains, avenues of trees, museums—we wanted that so-called city turned—as indeed it now has been—irreversibly to dust.

Now as for these children, the General found them in a drain, Amelia. And the General being what he is—what you and I both know him to be—I mean not just a soldier, but a man—and not just a man—a father—a husband. Being all those things, he has asked me—which is delicate, I realise—but asked me to bring these children who couldn't stand up for blood—who were slipping, Amelia, in that drain, barefoot on the blood, and on the pulverised bone of their brothers and sisters—has asked me to bring them to this house to remind us—to remind each one of us—of our common—I hope—humanity.

Pause.

Beautician They must be exhausted—look at them.

Housekeeper But where are they going to sleep? You can't just bring children into the house and expect / Amelia to—

Amelia Please. He's right. This is a very beautiful gesture on my husband's part, and I fully support it—is that understood? I want these children washed and given beds. I want them given thick sheets—cotton ones—white ones—and a light—they must have a light in the room—pink perhaps—and toys. Find them some of Jamie's old toys—but nothing frightening, please—no guns, no helicopters. And books. What kind of stories d'you like? (*Slight pause.*) I'm asking you a question, children. What kind of stories? (*Slight pause.*) Why won't they talk to me?

Jonathan You're distressed, Amelia. Why don't we deal with this / in the morning.

Amelia Distressed? I am not distressed, Jonathan, I am extremely happy. I simply want to know why they won't talk to me. I mean, the big one's obviously quite grown-up—aren't you—aren't you? What's your name? Why won't she talk to me?

Jonathan They don't read books.

Amelia Oh? Don't read books?

Jonathan No.

Amelia Then why did they have libraries?

Jonathan The libraries were used to conceal weapons.

Amelia You mean like the schools?—like / the fountains?

Jonathan Like the schools—yes. (*Slight pause.*) I am telling you the truth / Amelia.

Amelia Of course they read books—look at their eyes— they are intelligent. This one—this pretty one—look at her eyes. (*Slight pause.*) Or are you saying they don't speak English?

Jonathan They don't speak at all. They are unable to speak. They have been living in a drain, Amelia.

  Pause.

Amelia (*laughs*) Of course.

Jonathan Yes.

Amelia Forgive me.

Jonathan You are forgiven.

Amelia Please forgive me. So you don't think . . .

Jonathan Think what?

Amelia Nothing. (*to Girl*) Show me your tongue, sweetheart. Tongue. I want to see your tongue.

Jonathan Amelia?

  Amelia sticks her tongue right out over her lower lip and makes noises to encourage the Girl to show her tongue, if she has one. The Girl finally silently extends her tongue.

Amelia Thank god for that. (*Smiles.*) Well thank god for that.

Everyone, except for the Girl, smiles. Amelia takes hold of her affectionately.

Listen: you are very welcome in this house. Whatever has happened to you, I want you to know that you are now safe, you are now loved. D'you understand me?

Amelia and the Girl stare at each other. The Boy suddenly breaks away and, before the Housekeeper can grab him, presses a button on the stereo. The Billie Holiday track plays from where it was interrupted to the end.

THREE

Night. Close, but not overwhelming, a plane passes on its way to the airport. Faint light reveals Richard sitting drinking. A beam of light enters the room and settles on Richard's face: it's the Housekeeper, with a powerful torch. Next to her is Amelia, carrying the Boy. On account of the child, they all speak softly.

Amelia Still here?

Richard Amelia? What're you doing?

Amelia He was having nightmares. We went outside to look at the stars, but there weren't any.

Richard Please. That hurts my eyes.

Amelia Switch it off.

Housekeeper Why haven't you gone home?

Amelia Switch it off. Take him, would you—he's getting heavy.

Housekeeper takes the child and gives Amelia the switched-off torch.

Richard I wanted to talk to you, actually.

Housekeeper makes to go.

Amelia No. Stay. Well here I am: talk to me.

Richard I thought you deserved to be told the truth.

Amelia Oh?

Richard Yes.

Amelia Deserved?

Richard Yes.

Amelia (*faint laugh*) What truth? What does a man like you know / about truth?

Richard He's lying.

Amelia Mmm?

Richard Jonathan—he's lying.

Amelia Of course he's lying—it's war—it's his job / to lie.

Richard He's lying about the children—not about the war—well, yes, of course about the war—but also about the children. Because these children are not what he said: 'victims'—'survivors'. They are the spoils, Amelia. (*Grins.*)

We hear the Girl calling softly offtstage for the Boy: 'Edu . . . Edu . . .'

Amelia I don't understand.

Housekeeper He's drunk.

Amelia She's right—you're drunk—I want you / to leave.

Richard The oldest child—the girl—her name is Laela.

Amelia And?

Richard Give me the torch.

Amelia No.

Richard Give me the torch.

Amelia No.

A silent but intense struggle for the torch. Richard gets it, switches it on.

Richard Here come the helicopters. And here come the rockets out of the rocket-tubes. And here are the bottles of blood bursting in the hospital refrigerators. And oh—look—these are the patients blown off their beds onto the broken glass. And here are some heads on poles, Amelia . . .

Laela appears looking for the Boy.

Amelia Boring, boring—you think I don't / *know* all this?

Richard And here—oh look—what's this? What's this, Amelia? Who's this? Who's this girl? Her name is Laela. And he wants this girl so much—so much—he is so—what's the word?—inflamed—he is so—that's right—inflamed—that in order to take this girl from her father he is prepared to murder not just the father, but the inhabitants of an entire city . . .

Housekeeper Don't listen to him / Amelia.

Richard . . . of an entire city. Yes. Then ship the girl and what remains of her family . . . (*Shines beam at Amelia.*) . . . back to his own wife.

Pause. He snaps off the torch. The Boy whimpers. Laela goes to him.

Amelia What does he mean? What d'you mean? What're you trying to say to me?

24

Richard (*grins*) Don't think telling you this gives me any pleasure.

Amelia Get that child out, will you. Go on: *out*. Get it *out*.

The Housekeeper takes Laela and the Boy out.

Now. Explain.

Jonathan Explain what, Amelia?

Jonathan has appeared, mobile phone to his ear.

(*into phone*) Yup. Yup. I'm busy, sweetheart. Give me five more minutes, would you?

He ends the call but continues to scroll through messages without looking up.

Sorry—I'm needed elsewhere—explain what?

Amelia You're needed elsewhere.

Jonathan Yes—sorry—it's been one of / those nights.

Amelia I'm disappointed.

Jonathan Mmm?

Amelia I said: I'm disappointed—there were some questions I was hoping to ask.

Jonathan Questions—of course there are—why don't you call my office in / the morning?

Amelia Will you please look at me when I talk to you?

Jonathan Mmm?

He continues tapping at the phone, then looks up. He pockets the phone and smiles.

Amelia Who exactly are these children?

Jonathan Exactly? We're not in a position to say. They don't have papers.

Amelia But presumably they have names.

Jonathan Presumably their parents gave them names— I believe that is a universal habit. Why?

Amelia And who are their parents?

Jonathan I'm sorry?

Richard She's asking you who their / parents are.

Jonathan Their parents—I've explained this—are dead.

Richard Murdered.

Jonathan What?

Richard Their parents have been / murdered.

Jonathan Their parents have not been 'murdered', Richard—please grow up, please grow up—Seratawa was / a *terrorist*.

Richard So she's Seratawa's daughter.

Jonathan The children have no papers. Nothing at this stage can be confirmed. They were found—that's all—as I have already said—in a traumatised state—

Richard In a drain.

Jonathan Yes.

Richard Not in a palace, then.

Jonathan In a drain—in a palace—wherever they were found it was in a traumatised state, and I see no point in continuing / this conversation.

Richard Because I was told—oh, don't you? don't you?—
because I was told they were found beneath a palace. I
was told they were Seratawa's children.

Jonathan You were told.

Richard Yes, I was told by you. (*Slight pause.*) And I was
also told—unless this was a smear—was this a deliberate
smear?—because I was also told—as were others—that
the General's objectives were not so much military, as
sexual. That the assault—your word, not mine—was a
sexual one.

   Slight pause.

Jonathan You have a sick sick mind, my friend. Amelia,
I think you've been distressed enough for one evening.
I'll take / him home.

Amelia
   If you call me distressed
   Jonathan
   one more time
   or use my name
   Jonathan
   one more time tonight I won't scream
   no
   what I will in fact do
   is stuff your mouth with barbed wire.
   Because forgive me
   but I'm starting to find the way you speak
   an atrocity which makes cutting a man's heart out
   seem almost humane.
   If you have something to say
   about that child and my husband
   say it. But don't and I repeat
   don't think you can what?
   'spare my feelings?'

because I am not a child
and do not expect to be treated like a child
in my own house—is that clear?
You think it's a secret
that my husband has other women?
You think he doesn't tell me about them?
Oh yes—oh yes—he tells me about them—
their names
the colour of their hair—
because he knows I'd rather be told
even if being told is
and it is
I can promise you that it is
like having my face sprayed with acid.
When I slept with you
Jonathan
I told him the same evening
and after he'd punched his fist through the bathroom
    wall
he made me put on my red dress
and took me dancing.
Whereas—let me guess—you and
Kitty?—was that Kitty on the phone?—yes?—Kitty?—
Kitty and yourself—poor little Kitty
has never been told, has she,
even though her ignorance
is precisely what you despise about her—
am I right?

Slight pause.

You see
Jonathan
I happen to believe that love and truth
are the same thing.

Jonathan Your indiscretion appals me.

Amelia Oh, does it? I'm so sorry.

Jonathan All I am doing in a very very difficult situation here is trying to / protect you.

Amelia It's true, then.

Jonathan What?

Amelia What Richard says: what Richard / says is true.

Jonathan Nobody is trying to smear the General, no.

Amelia In other words it's true.

Jonathan (*to Richard*) You have no right to imply that.

Amelia Meaning it's true.

Jonathan Apparently.

Amelia I didn't hear you. What?

Jonathan I said apparently—yes—alright?—it's true.

Amelia bursts out laughing.

Amelia And you believe that?

Jonathan Yes.

Amelia That he would massacre a what?—an entire / *population?*—

Jonathan The evidence points that way.

Amelia 'The evidence points that way'—oh really?—does it?—for this *person?*—for this . . . *child?*

Richard Hardly a child, sweetheart.

Amelia stops laughing.

Jonathan Listen—

Amelia I don't believe it.

Jonathan Listen—

29

Amelia You're just trying to damage him—no.

Jonathan Amelia—

Amelia DON'T YOU DARE PUT YOUR HAND ON ME.

Slight pause.

Jonathan (*calmly*) I have no wish to damage anyone—least of all yourself. I have to leave now. I suggest—and this is simply a suggestion—suggest that you go to bed—that you try to sleep—and that in the morning you call my office—excuse me.

He turns away to answer his mobile.

Hello?
Where are you?
Uh-hu. Uh-hu. I see.
In the house.
I said in the house, I'm in the house.
(*meeting Amelia's eyes*) Asleep I think.
Uh-hu. Uh-hu. Okay. I'll try. One moment.

He takes the phone from his ear.

It's the General.

Amelia (*overjoyed*) Well, give me the phone. Where is he? (*Slight pause.*) What's wrong with you? Give me the phone.

Jonathan He's on a plane. He's asking to speak to Laela.*

---

*In the original production there was a struggle for the phone. When Amelia got hold of it, the General's voice was audible: *Laela?—Laela?—Don't be frightened: it's me.—It's me sweetheart.—Come on, Laela: talk to me.—Laela?—Sweetheart?—Laela?—Laela?*

Part Two

ONE

Some days later, Laela, exactly like Amelia in the earlier scene, is being given beauty treatment by the Beautician and Physiotherapist. Following the words with her finger, she reads aloud from a women's magazine.

The Housekeeper plays quietly with the Boy.

Laela (*reads*) 'Tell him how you want to be touched. Tell him what your . . .' (*Shows word.*)

Physiotherapist Fantasies.

Laela '. . . what your fantasies are. Don't feel . . . ashamed. If your man doesn't touch you the way you like, give your man a lesson. You may want to . . .' (*Shows word.*)

Physiotherapist Masturbate.

Laela '. . . masturbate in front of each other. Many . . .' (*Shows word.*) Couples?

Physiotherapist Very good.

Laela 'Many couples find this leads to better sex. Remember there is no right or wrong. You are an . . .' (*Shows word.*) . . . indian?

Physiotherapist Individual.

Laela '. . . an individual, and every . . . individual expresses love in their own individual way.'

Beautician That's very good, Laela. Did you learn English at school?

Laela Only boys go to school. I learn English at Tuseme club. (*Turns page.*) Oh, look at this dress! I want this dress!

Beautician What's Tuseme club?

Laela Tuseme club is HIV Aids learning club. You think he'll buy me this dress?

Physiotherapist Only if you're nice to him.

Laela Oh, I'm always nice to him.

The girls all laugh. Amelia appears. They go quiet.

Amelia What's that round your neck, Laela?

Physiotherapist You'd left it in the bathroom.

Amelia I've told you: she's not to take my things.

Housekeeper She doesn't mean any harm.

Amelia I'm sure. (*Smiles, holds out her hand.*) Laela?

After a pause, Laela unfastens the necklace she's wearing and gives it to Amelia. She continues to look at the magazine.

Don't you miss your family? (*Slight pause.*) I said: don't you miss / your family?

Laela My father was bad. He took the rice.

Amelia Oh?

Laela He took the rice out of people's mouths. And if he saw a man swallow the rice, he'd put his own hand into the man's body and pull the rice out again. (*Grins.*)

Amelia Your mother, then?

Laela I miss the General. When is he coming home? I want him to buy this dress.

Amelia The General is my husband, Laela. D'you understand what that means?

Laela One man can have many wives.

Amelia Of course, of course—but here—where you are now—when a man marries a woman, he stays with that woman.

Laela Just her?

Amelia That's what marriage is.

Laela (*laughs*) I don't believe you. That's what they tell girls at Tuseme club.

Amelia It's the truth.

Laela A man can have two wives under one blanket.

Amelia No. Not here. No.

Laela You mean he has to choose.

Amelia What I mean—Laela—is that the choice has already been made. I am his choice. I am the mother of his child. When he wakes up in the bed screaming, I am the person who switches on the light, and fetches the glass of water. (*Sees the Boy has a toy gun.*) What's this? I thought I said no guns. (*No one speaks.*) I said no guns.

Housekeeper It's only a toy, Amelia.

Amelia But I specifically / asked.

Laela (*soft*) Boys need to fight.

Amelia What did you say?

Laela (*with growing intensity*) Boys need to fight—they need to learn—they need to kill. Boys need to kill. Boys need to fight. Boys must fight. Boys must kill—must learn to kill. Boys need to fight—they need to learn—they need

33

to kill. Boys need to kill. Boys need to fight. Boys must
fight. Boys must kill—must learn to kill. Boys need to—

*Amelia hits Laela. Laela for a moment is stunned—
then leaves the room. The Boy runs out after her.*

*Long pause. Housekeeper, Physiotherapist and
Beautician watch Amelia, warily.*

*Suddenly Amelia points toy gun at Physiotherapist,
who instinctively raises her arms. She smiles.*

After we married—
did I ever tell you this?—
he was immediately sent away
into the desert
and I was bored.

She tosses gun into the toy-box.

I was so bored that I called
this boy I'd known at university
who'd spent his years at university
marching for peace
and when not marching for peace
shut in a lab. He was a chemist
and despised my husband.
Anyway I called him
and I said 'How are you?' he said
'I'm living in the country
come to the station and I'll collect you'
so I got the train
and he collected me from the country station
and without the beard
he was actually quite attractive.
I said 'This is a nice car, Robert' he said
'Yes, it comes with the job' I said
'What job?' he said 'I'll show you'.

She begins to unpick the stitches of a pillow.

So he drove me past these meadows
with rabbits and things—pheasants—
scuttling away to their holes
until we reached a beech-lined drive
which led to the facility
a kind of low concrete facility
a concrete and in fact windowless—yes—facility
where Robert
who'd spent his years at university
marching for peace
had been given a budget
staff and a number of caged dogs
and a number of caged primates
—macaques, were they?—
to develop weapons.

He showed me the park.
He knew the names of the wild flowers
flowers I hadn't even noticed
until he separated the grass where we were lying
and broke off the white stars.
I was so young! Next to the stream I did
of course I did the predictable things he wanted
except—because I was pregnant now—
let him touch me.

But the thing is
what I'm trying to say is
is on that day at the facility
he gave me this

She produces a glass tube the size of a pen-top.

which he said was his 'baby'.
He told me that this
whatever it is

chemical
that this chemical
his baby
took the will to fight out of a soldier
by making the soldier yearn for a safe place
making him feel the need of a safe place
an absolute need
for the love and the reassurance
of the person he was closest to.
Humane
was the word he used
to describe his baby.
I know it sounds mad
but I believed him.

Slight pause.

(*Laughs.*) Don't look at me like that.

Housekeeper Like what, Amelia?

Amelia Like I'm out of / my mind.

Beautician It's probably just water. Show me.

Physiotherapist Does it smell?

Beautician It smells of scent.

Amelia That's from the drawer. I keep it in my perfume drawer.

Beautician How does it open?

Amelia It doesn't: you have to break the glass.

Housekeeper And he called it humane.

Amelia Yes. Why not?

Physiotherapist Weird.

Slight pause.

Beautician Amelia. Catch.

*Beautician tosses the tube to Amelia who—terrified—
catches it.*

Amelia Idiot.

*Housekeeper, Physiotherapist and Beautician laugh.
Ignoring them, Amelia carefully inserts the tube inside
the pillow.*

Jonathan appears.

Jonathan What's the joke, ladies?

Amelia Come here.

Jonathan Oh?

Amelia Come here. Come on. Closer. Closer.

*She kisses him at length. As she does so, Laela
appears, holding a wet flannel to her face, and
watches like the others.*

Jonathan And what have I done to deserve that?

Amelia You're going to be my messenger.

Jonathan Oh? What's the message?

Amelia You're going to explain how nice I've been to
the children—particularly to Laela.

Jonathan Uh-hu.

Amelia Because you've seen—you've all seen—yes?—how
generously I've accepted the situation.

Jonathan Uh-hu. And?

Amelia And nothing.

He tries to move away. She stops him.

Oh yes: one other thing.
You're flying out to the camp
to pin medals on the boys
and to support my husband—yes?
Well listen
to remind him of home
to help him sleep before he finally comes home
I have a white pillow
I want you to take out to him.
Tell him to think of me.
Tell him to push his face
into the soft part of the white pillow
and his mouth
and his tongue
tell him to push his whole face into the white pillow
     until
he feels something smooth and hard inside the white
     pillow
snap.

Slight pause.

Will you do that, Jonathan?

Jonathan It will take up space.

Amelia His tongue?

Jonathan The pillow, Amelia.

Amelia You have power. *Make* space.

During the preceding speech she has allowed Jonathan to touch her. Now she gently removes his hand.

Music: 1936 recording of Billie Holiday singing 'I Can't Give You Anything But Love'.

The messenger
Jonathan
must not be distracted from the message.

TWO

Evening. Music from previous scene continues uninter-
rupted as Housekeeper, Physiotherapist and Beautician
prepare the room for the General's return.

Voice of Billie Holiday
  I can't give you anything but love
  baby.
  That's the only thing I've plenty of
  baby.
  Scheme a while
  dream a while
  you're sure to find
  happiness
  and I guess
  all those things you've always pined for.

  Gee I'd like to see you looking swell
  baby.
  Diamond bracelets Woolworth's doesn't sell
  baby.

  Until that lucky day
  you know darn well
  baby
  I can't give you anything but love.

Amelia enters in the red dress she mentioned previously.
Her hair is elegant. She inspects the room. She turns
off the music.

Amelia Zip me up will you.

Beautician attempts to zip up the dress.

  Oh by the way
  I think something's happened to one of the children.

39

Yes I think
well no not think I know
that something's happened to one of those children.
I told them not to touch my things.
You heard me—didn't you—say that
say 'don't touch my things'.
But one of them's been in my drawer
been poking their fingers into my perfume drawer
had all my perfume out
had the whole drawer out and / broken it.

Housekeeper Wrong with them?

Amelia What?

Housekeeper You said something happened?

Amelia Hurry up with this zip can't you?

Beautician It's tight.

Amelia It's meant to be tight—it's a / tight dress.

Housekeeper Happened to who? Laela?

Amelia What? No. The little one. It got something on its fingers and stopped breathing—you're hurting me.

Beautician Sorry.

Physiotherapist Stopped breathing?

Amelia You're hurting me—be careful.

Physiotherapist What d'you mean it / stopped breathing?

Amelia Oh nothing, nothing—leave me alone!

The zip is finally done up. Amelia smoothes the dress over her hips.

I told you:
one moment it was poking around in the drawer

and the next it momentarily
just momentarily stopped breathing.
It's fine—it's had a strawberry yoghurt—
it's watching TV—it's fine—
Laela washed its hands
and put it in front of the TV
with a packet of crisps and a yoghurt
and it's absolutely fine—I swear to you.
And of course we've looked in the drawer:
Laela's looked—I've looked—we've both—
well of course we've both of us
had that drawer completely to pieces
and looked and looked
but apart from the splinters of wood
there's nothing—Laela agrees—
she agrees with me
there's nothing in the drawer that could've made this
    happen.
So why should I feel afraid?
Mmm?
I have to ask myself—you see—
exactly why this thing this
whatever it is this
coincidence—yes—obviously—but why this
coincidence is frightening me.
And of course once I start asking myself that question
I start thinking about Robert and Robert's friends:
all Robert's friends at university
with their tobacco tins.
I keep seeing the little shreds
of dry tobacco in their tobacco tins
and the grey light in the stairwells
of their squatted apartments where they planned
—what?—to 'overthrow the state'
'kill the pigs' blah blah blah
'liberate'—by which they meant fuck—

women—all that shit—all that liberate
liberate and overthrow the state shit
so that when a banker got shot say
taking his kids to school
or if an army officer
burned alive in a nightclub explosion
or if some boy
some soldier even younger than they were
who had been defending their right
to despise their expensive education
came home on TV in a body-bag
that didn't even contain his whole body
they'd find that oh yes they'd find that not just
acceptable
but exhilarating.
So what if Robert never grew up?
What if he'd cut his hair and taken that job
out of perversity?
What if for him this word 'humane'
was a sick joke?
(*Smiles.*) Tell me I'm wrong.
Tell me he didn't calculate that one day
he would make me responsible for treating my
   husband
like a monkey in an experiment.

Housekeeper Well of course you're wrong.

Amelia What time is it?

Physiotherapist Nine.

Amelia Who's called? Has anyone called?

Housekeeper You're tired. You're imagining things.

Amelia Oh am I?

Housekeeper Of course you are.

Amelia You see that is exactly what I would *expect* to be told by a person with no imagination.

James Nice dress, Mum.

Amelia Jamie?

James has appeared, holding the pillow he took when he left: now dirty and torn. Amelia puts her arms round him. James does not respond.

(*Smiles.*) Look at you. I thought you were your father.

James No Mum, I'm not my father.

Amelia Don't you think? Doesn't he look exactly like / his father?

Housekeeper Where is your father, Jamie?

James Delayed. (*Grins.*)

Slight pause.

Shall we eat something?

Amelia I'm sorry?

James I said shall we eat something, Mum—I'm / hungry.

Amelia What's wrong with you? What's wrong with your eyes?

James I'm hungry. I've been travelling. I'd like to eat. Nothing's wrong with my eyes—I'm just tired and hungry. (*Grins.*) Nice dress.

Slight pause.

Amelia You just / said that.

James Maybe a bit tight.

Amelia What?

James Tight. Maybe a / bit tight.

43

Amelia That's the style. It's a tight style.

James It's a tight style.

Amelia Yes.

James Wine?

Amelia What?

James Wine?

Amelia Yes please.

He pours Amelia a glass of wine.

James Well, come on, Mum—drink it.

Amelia Aren't you having any?

James Come on.

Housekeeper Ignore him, Amelia.

James I beg your pardon?

Beautician Leave your mum alone, James.

James Fuck off, bitch.

Amelia Jamie?

James Don't you tell me what to do in my own house. I want all three of you out of this room now and I want you to take that pillow and I want you to fucking clean it. Go on—out. Drink the wine, Mum. (*She begins to drink.*) All of it.

As Housekeeper, Physiotherapist and Beautician leave the room, Amelia drinks the glass of wine. James immediately refills it.

Well don't you want to hear about Africa?

Amelia Of course I do—how was / Africa?

James Africa? Africa was great, Mum. On Sunday mornings the church bells ring and all the Africans get into their African jeeps and drive to church under the autumn leaves.

Amelia Oh?

James And in the afternoons—what?—does that surprise you?—because in the afternoons, while their parents are assembling flat-pack African furniture with hexagonal keys, the kids hang out in the Mexican restaurants or experiment with sex or with rocket-propelled grenades— more wine, Mum?

   Slight pause.

Amelia I didn't realise that they—

James That they what, Mum? Had Mexican food?

Amelia Had autumn—had autumn leaves.

James You see, at first I blamed the Mexican cuisine. Because I wake up and I can hear Dad vomiting in the bathroom and naturally I think it's the Mexican cuisine, Mum—that Tex-Mex African pizza—that snake-meat enchilada dished up at the victory celebration in the officers' canteen—but no. No, Mum—it's not the food— that's not why my father—who can walk into fire, remember—walk into fire to drag out a wounded soldier and walk with that wounded soldier on his back for ten hours across sand—that's not why my father is in that bathroom gripping both sides of the sink the way an old man trying to get to the post office holds on to his walking-frame. That's not why he's sucking in air—sucking and sucking in the air, Mum, like he's drowning in his own spit.

And there's this thing on his back, Mum—no—not on his back but under it—this thing under his skin—like an animal under his skin—it's crawling—it's crawling under his skin—like an animal, Mum, trying to slide out from underneath—which is the chemical—the animal under the skin—the pain—the chemical—the thing your friend brought—the gift—the gift / your friend brought—

Amelia He's not my friend. / Stop this.

James —the gift of pain—the chemical—your chemical under the skin. (*Slight pause.*) And when he turns round it's his eyes—it's worked its way up his spine and into his eyes—he's got these eyes like a cat in the sun—pin-point eyes—he isn't human, Mum—that's what you and your friend have done to him—

Amelia Stop it.

James —not even human. Which is why when he talks to me—when he says 'It's going dark: give me your hand'—when he says 'Help me, help me, give me your fucking hand' there is no way I am going to let this person—no—sorry—thing—no way I am going to let this thing with the pin-point fucking eyes that used to be my dad even *touch* me.

Then it's TV drama, Mum. It's straight-to-video medical-emergency bullshit:
   'Chemical attack' blah blah blah.
   'Atropine ten milligrams.'
   'Oxygen.'
   'Ventilate.' (*He grins.*)

So perhaps you would like to finish this glass of wine and explain to me why you have killed my father.

He pours wine into her glass, making it overflow. Amelia tries to stop him. The glasses smash.

Laughter: Housekeeper, Physiotherapist and Beautician, dressed up for an evening out, can be seen leaving the house.

Beautician (*calls*) 'Night, Amelia! 'Night, Jamie!

Housekeeper (*calls*) Back door's locked. Remember those children are still watching TV. Amelia?

Beautician Don't bother—she's not listening.

Physiotherapist Love those shoes.

Beautician Found them in her wardrobe—don't / tell anyone.

Housekeeper (*calls*) Make sure those children / get to bed.

Physiotherapist Let's just get out of here. Come on. Sweet dreams, Jamie.

Beautician Shh. Stop it.

Laughing and joking, the three women leave. Pause. James continues to stare at Amelia.

Amelia (*softly*) Nicola? Rachel? (*louder*) Rachel? I want you.

James They've gone, Mum.

Amelia (*calls out*) I want this mess cleared up. I want these things put away immediately. Rachel! Cathy!

James There's nobody here—they all / went out.

Amelia (*calls out*) Nicola! Rachel! Clear up this mess!

James They've left, Mum. There's nobody here. I am waiting for your / explanation.

Amelia Africa sounds lovely. I hope you took photographs. I'd love to see those leaves—and all the restaurants—I'd no idea—I thought it was all idleness and destruction—(*Calls.*) Laela?

47

James You know nothing, Mum: and that is because your life is entirely devoid of content. You don't even leave / the *house*.

Amelia (*calls*) Laela!

James It's like you live in a / *bunker*.

Amelia Laela! Turn off that / television and come in here!

James Africa? It's not Africa that's idle and destructive, Mum, it's you. Don't you understand / what you've done?

Amelia (*smiles*) Sweetheart. There you are. I'd like you to meet my son.

Laela has appeared. Slight pause.

Well, come on. Come on, Laela: meet my son.

She grips Laela's hand and pulls her into the room.

Laela, this is James. Jamie, this is Laela. What d'you think, James? As a man. Is she worth it? You don't need to look so blank—I'm asking you if she's worth it—well?

James You're hurting her.

Amelia Is that right? Am I hurting you, sweetheart?

Laela No.

Amelia You see: Laela says no. Laela's used to pain. She's used to dismemberment and death. Laela doesn't need you to explain to me how Laela feels. Do you, Laela?

Laela No.

Amelia How d'you feel, Laela?

Slight pause.

48

Laela I feel good.

Amelia You see: Laela feels good. So what d'you say, Jamie? Worth it? Come on. You're a man. You can judge. How many people would *you* kill?

James I don't understand. Who are you? What's she doing / in the house?

Amelia Don't you? Don't you? Well maybe you're not a man at all then. What do *you* say, Laela? Is this a man? Is it? A person who thinks it's—what?—brave is it, to come here and terrorise his mother? A person who is too frightened—by his own admission—Laela—is too frightened to take his *own dying father's hand*?

James backs away.

No—Jamie—I'm sorry—I'm very very sorry—please—please—that was wrong of me—please.

James goes out. In the silence, a plane passes. Then:

Laela I turned off the TV.

Amelia Mmm?

Laela I turned off / the TV.

Amelia Thank you, Laela.

Laela I'm sorry about the drawer.

Amelia The drawer doesn't matter.

Laela I will punish the boy.

Amelia Did he eat his yoghurt?

Laela Yes, but he spit out the fruit.

Amelia Spat, Laela—spat out the fruit.

Pause.

Can you drive a car?

49

Laela Can I . . .?

Amelia Drive. Can you drive a car?

Laela No.

Amelia Neither can I. If we could drive a car, we could drive to the airport. We could go shopping at the airport. What d'you think?

Laela Buy shoes.

Amelia We could buy shoes. We could buy luggage on wheels.

Pause.

What have I done, Laela?

Laela What have you . . .?

Amelia DONE. WHAT HAVE I DONE?

Pause.

Laela Can we really go to the airport?

Amelia Of course we can, sweetheart. But first you're going to pour me a glass of wine. Let's have a glass of wine together, shall we? Then what we'll do is we'll take the General's car and we'll drive to the airport and meet the General—yes? The two wives will drive to the airport in their husband's car to collect their husband from the airport—what d'you think? Good idea? Everybody drives—it can't be / difficult.

Laela It's broken.

Amelia Even really stupid stupid people drive a car—what?

Laela These glasses / are broken.

Amelia Then fetch some more.

Laela goes out.

I know what we can do, Laela:
how about we put ourselves—mmm?—
through the machines—
what d'you say?
How about we lie down on the rubber track
and ask to be X-rayed
because obviously
there's obviously something inside of us
Laela
some sharp object
some spike
something inside of us
a prohibited object we didn't know about
but that will show up on the screen close
because I think it must be very close to our hearts
—don't you think?—that spike?
So they'll ask us to strip.
And when we've stripped
(which I hope we will do like grown-ups without
    complaining)
one of those women with a rubber-glove
will push her hand
like a midwife Laela
will push her hand deeper and deeper into us
until the tip of her finger rests
just so
on the spike.

Laela reappears, holding glasses.

And she'll say
'I suspect you of terror.
You have a concealed weapon.
I can feel it next to your heart.'
'Oh really?' I'll say 'D'you mean love?'

And she'll say 'Not love
no
I'm talking about this spike.
Have you concealed this spike deliberately?
Or could it have been placed there
without your knowledge?'
And I'll lie to her
I'll say 'Deliberately of course.'
Because otherwise
I could be mistaken for a victim
and that's not a part
Laela
that I'm prepared to play.

Amelia clenches her fist around one of the shattered wine-glasses and squeezes as hard as she can. When she finally opens it, some of the glass drops out, some remains sticking to her hand.

(*Smiles.*) Let's look for the car keys. We're driving to the airport.

Part Three

A month later. Saturday morning.

Beauty treatment: the Housekeeper is having the finger-nails of her right hand painted by the Beautician, while the Physiotherapist sits apart, leafing through a women's magazine.

There's a new object in the room: a small stainless-steel trolley containing items (cotton-wool pads, bottle of alcohol, medication, towels, thermometer, plastic gloves etc.) to care for an invalid. There may also be a wheelchair, and perhaps a bowl of fruit.

Housekeeper
Hairbrush.
Lamp.
Light-switch.
Doors—naturally.
The bed.
Bathroom mirror.
Bathroom sink.
Bathroom towels.
Telephone.
Medicine cabinet and all inside the medicine cabinet—
naturally.

Beautician (*faint laugh*) That's revolting.

Housekeeper
Well, you asked.
Jewellery box.

Beautician Don't.

Housekeeper
Jewellery box.
Toothbrush.

Physiotherapist Toothbrush?

Housekeeper
Toothbrush: that's what I said.
Toothbrush.
Hairbrush.
The bed.
The pillow.
Nightdress under the pillow—pure silk—ruined.
Oh, and underwear.
The underwear drawer.
Edge of the kitchen table.
Wall of the passageway.
Door—naturally—door to the garage.
Garage light-switch.
Wall around the light-switch.
Car windscreen.
The inside as well as the outside of the glass.
Car keys.
Mirror.

Pause. She examines her free hand.

What are these ridges in my fingernails?

Beautician Stress does that. They grow out.

Housekeeper I hope so.

Physiotherapist So you had to clear it all up?

Housekeeper What? The blood? No. That's what I'm saying. They told me to leave it. 'Don't touch anything. This is a crime scene.'

Physiotherapist Even the toothbrush?

Housekeeper Well exactly—it's not a crime to brush your teeth—it's not a crime to be broken-hearted. Is it?

Beautician Keep your hand still.

Housekeeper Well, is it? And they're asking me where I've been—why wasn't I in the house? And I say, 'Well it's my night off.' And they go, 'Just tell us where you've been.' So I tell them where I've been: I've been to the Star of Izmir. 'What's that?' So I explain it's an all-night Turkish restaurant close to the North Terminal, hotbed of international terrorism.

Physiotherapist (*laughs*) You didn't.

Housekeeper I most certainly did, Cathy—because these people are starting to make me very angry. They're all over the house like flies on a plate of ham, and of course I've got Jamie acting more like a six-year-old than an adult, blaming himself as if that that was any use because they'd had some kind of argument about the thing that happened to his father and he'd stormed out apparently and left her. Is this finished? (*i.e. nails*)

Beautician Uh-hu.

Housekeeper (*getting up and admiring her fingernails*) Because he's the one you see who saw the light on in the garage windows—I really like this colour: thank you—he saw the light on but it wasn't until he realised she was running the engine that it dawned on him what might be happening. And by the time he'd got the doors open, it was too late. There she was—hair all brushed—curled up on the back seat like a baby.

Slight pause.

What is this colour called?

Beautician Spangled Night.

Housekeeper It's lovely.

Physiotherapist He looks nice in a suit, though.

Housekeeper I'm sorry?

Physiotherapist Jamie—looks really nice in / a suit.

Housekeeper He's certainly had some growing up to do, if that's what you mean.

Beautician So what is it they're talking about in there?

Housekeeper (*lowers voice*) What they're talking about is responsibility. Not about suits, Cathy, but about assuming responsibility. (*softer and softer*) And I would ask both you girls to remember that as far as we are concerned . . . this is a *perfectly normal day.* Understood?

> *Offstage the General can be heard approaching, half speaking, half singing.* *

I am asking you if that is understood.

Beautician Normal day. Fine.

Housekeeper Cathy? (*Slight pause.*) Cathy?

Physiotherapist Yes alright, it's a normal day.

General (*off, sings/speaks without expression*) 'I can't give you anything but love—baby. That's the only thing I've plenty of—baby. Scheme a while. Dream a while. You're sure to find—happiness—and I guess—'

> *The General appears, dressed in a tracksuit, and halts mid-phrase. The women look at him warily. He surveys the room. He smiles.*

Ladies. Good morning.

Housekeeper *and* **Beautician** Good morning, General.

---

*In the original production the General was present from the beginning of the scene, asleep, naked.

56

Physiotherapist How are you today?

General I feel good.

Pause. Without moving, he continues to survey the room.

Housekeeper D'you need emptying, General?

General Do I need what?

Housekeeper (*softly*) Empty his bag, Nicola.

General (*to Housekeeper*)
Now listen:
tell Amelia we're having lunch at the Chinese Embassy
then at three o'clock
put this in the diary
because at three o'clock
I'm talking to the minister about helicopters
because there are not enough helicopters
and I have men dying because of it and then at half
  past four
this should be in the diary
at half past four I am appearing on television
until half past five when a car is taking Amelia and
  myself
and make sure this car is booked
because we need to go directly to the airport
for a meeting at the United Nations in New York.
So you will kindly tell Amelia
that after lunch at the Chinese Embassy
she must come home and pack
and I will need the adaptor for my razor
because the voltage in New York is not the same is it?

Slight pause.

I am asking you a question.

*During the preceding speech Beautician has wheeled
the trolley over to the General, knelt to pull down his
jogging-pants, revealing a urine-bag strapped to his
leg, drained the bag into a jug and pulled the pants
back up again. On his last line he grips her by the hair.*

Beautician What question, General?

General What is the voltage in New York?

Beautician You're hurting me.

General I'm doing what?

Housekeeper (*calmly*) Let go of her hair. Please. She
doesn't know the answer.

General (*releasing her*) Doesn't know the answer.

Beautician No—sorry.

General I've hurt you.

Beautician I'm used to it.

General Pain?

Beautician Yes.

General (*smiles*) Used to pain? Oh really?

Slight pause.

And you are . . . ?

Beautician You know who I am. I'm Nicola.

General You're fucking my son.

Beautician No.

General You're the one fucking my son.

Beautician No.

General Which one of you is fucking my son, then?

58

Slight pause. He looks at them. Points at
Physiotherapist.

This one.

Housekeeper (*to distract him*) Three o'clock, General?

General This is the one: look at her.

Housekeeper Three o'clock? Yes?

General This is the one. This is the one who shrieks in the night—like a fox—shrieks like / a fox.

Housekeeper Three o'clock?

General What?

Housekeeper At three o'clock you're talking to the minister—remember—about / helicopters.

General
    At three o'clock I'm talking to the minister
    that's right
    about helicopters because there are not enough
    helicopters and at half past four
    put this in the diary
    I am appearing on television until—

The General experiences an intense pain which
momentarily stops him speaking. To master the pain
he counts back in sevens:

One hundred and three . . . ninety-six . . . eighty-nine . . . eighty-two . . .

Physiotherapist General?

Beautician Keep back—don't touch him.

General . . . seventy-five . . . sixty-eight . . . (*Pain eases.*) sixty-one . . . and so on . . . (*Smiles.*) to infinity.

Slight pause.

Get me my son. I want to see my son—where is he?

Housekeeper James can't come. He's busy.

General I want to talk to him.

Beautician He's in a meeting.

General (*amused*) My son is in a meeting? What meeting?

Housekeeper Nicola just means there are people he has to / talk to.

General GET ME MY SON, SOLDIER.

> *Housekeeper gestures to Physiotherapist, who leaves the room.*

(*paranoid*) Where's she going?

Housekeeper She's gone to get James.

General She's going to talk to the government.

Housekeeper She's gone to find James, that's all.

General Don't let her talk to / the government.

Beautician (*to distract him*) Shall we tidy you up, General? Mmm? Shall we make you look nice?—for the television?

General (*stares at her*)
D'you think I'm a child, Nicola?
Or maybe you think
is this what you think?
that I'm losing my mind?
that a chemical has made me lose my mind?
that because of that bitch
I felt the glass crack in the white pillow
is this what you think?
that the glass cracked in the white pillow and I lost

my mind? Because I wake up on a Saturday morning
smelling of my own shit
that makes me an imbecile?

James appears in suit, unseen by the General.

Well, does it? (*Smiles.*) Maybe you'd like me to call for
fire, Nicola.

Beautician Don't know what you mean.

General
    Call for fire
    give your co-ordinates and call for fire.
    Then you won't doubt the accuracy of my mind.
    Because my mind is accurate to one square metre
      anywhere
    on the surface of this earth.
    And if I call for fire
    Nicola
    you will quite simply turn into a stick of flame.

*Attack of pain. General counts as before. James
indicates to Housekeeper and Beautician to leave.
They go out.*

One hundred and five . . . ninety-eight . . . ninety-one . . .
eighty-four . . . seventy-seven . . . (*Pain eases.*) seventy-
seven . . . seventy . . . sixty-three—

James (*cold*) What d'you want, Dad?

General Mmm?

James What is it you want?

General (*simply*) I want you to find me the bitch.

James What bitch, Dad?

General The bitch that did this to me—the bitch that
poisoned me—bring the bitch here.

James I'm not listening, Dad.

61

General Bring the bitch here. I want to break her legs.

James Don't use that word about my mother.

General Break her legs for me. I want to see her dance.

James I've told you: she's dead.

General Poison her the way she poisoned me.

James I've told you: she's dead.

General *Then* watch her dance—let's see her try and dance.

James You have seen her buried: you stood next to me.

  Pause.

General Died how?

James I've told you this.

General Killed.

James Yes.

General (*paranoid*) Killed by the government—murdered by the government.

James No, Dad—killed herself.

General Murdered by the government.

James Will you please listen to me: Amelia is dead. She killed herself. She killed herself because of you.

General (*smiles, flattered*) Me? Oh? Because of me?

James You have known this for a month now.

  Pause. James makes to leave.

I'm sorry, Dad, but I have to go.

General Back to your meeting.

James What?

General You have to go back to your / meeting.

James Who told you that?

General Who are you talking to?

James I'm not talking to anyone.

General You're talking to the government.

James I talk to who I like, Dad. I live in this house and I talk to who I like and there is something you need to understand: you are a criminal. You are accused of crimes. You have wiped people off this earth like a teacher rubbing out equations. You've stacked up bodies like bags of cement.

General (*smiles*) Is this what you learn at the university?

James I'm not listening, Dad.

General To hate your father—to spit in your own / father's face.

James I said I'm not / listening.

General
    Because I have purified the world for you.
    I have burnt terror out of the world for people like you.
    I have followed it through the shopping malls
    and the school playgrounds
    tracked it by starlight across the desert
    smashed down the door of its luxury apartment
    learned its language
    intercepted its phone calls
    smoked it out of its cave
    thrown acid into its eyes and burned it to carbon.
    While you've been logged on to internet chat-rooms
    I've seen my friends burst open like fruit.
    While you were hiding your face in that girl's hair—
    yes?—yes?—

I have been breathing in uranium.
Every streak of vapour in a cold sky
is a threat
every child with no shoes
wandering up to a checkpoint
every green tree-line
every quiet evening spent reading
is a threat
and even the lamp on the bedside table
even the coiled filament inside the lamp
is a threat.
So don't you talk to me about crimes
because for every head I have ever severed
two have grown in their place
and I have had to cut and to cut and to cut
to burn and to cut to purify the world—
understand me?
(*softly*) I killed the Nemean lion
oh yes—
with these hands—with these hands—
and the dog
the dog with the three heads
I collected it from hell in front of the cameras
I have visited the dead in front of the cameras—
remember?
(*Points to himself proudly.*) *Kallinikos. Kallinikos.*

Pause.

James Yes, Dad.

General (*tenderly*) Tell me something: where is my son?

James I am your son.

General You?

James Yes Dad.

General Then why are you doing that?

James Doing what?

General Why are you backing away from me?

James I'm not.

General My son wouldn't back away from me. Where is my son?

James I am your son.

General James—Jamie.

James Yes.

General But where is the other one? Where is my little one? The one from Gisenyi.

    Slight pause.

James (*in disbelief*) Fuck off.

General Where is my little one?

James Fuck off, Dad—that isn't true.

General I want to see him. I want to see Laela.

James That's not true, Dad. That boy is her brother.

General I want to see my son.

James I am your son—I am your only son—that isn't true.

General You are my only son?

James Yes.

General Then tell me something: why is it so quiet here? When is the attack?

James You're at home, Dad.

General I know where I am. And I know what's it's like before the attack. Sometimes it's so quiet you can hear the ants running over your boots. (*Smiles.*)

James (*turning away*) I have to go.

General James—Jamie—my only son.

James That's right.

General Then if you love me promise me something. You must promise to talk to the doctors. You will tell the doctors to help me die. You will not allow me to be humiliated. You will talk to the doctors and the doctors will help me die.

   Slight pause.

James I can't do that.

General Why? Don't you love your father?

James Of course I love my father—but I also love justice.

General (*smiles*) Justice.

James Yes.

General This is justice.

James Yes—no—no—not this, but—

General But what? To lose my mind?

James You're not losing your mind. You know precisely what you've done.

General I have only ever done what I was instructed to do. And what I was instructed to do . . . (*Becomes uncertain.*) . . . what I was instructed to do . . . This should be in the diary . . . put this in the diary . . .

   Slight pause. James observes his father.

James (*cold*) I'll talk to the doctors. Not help you die— I can't be responsible, obviously, for that—but I can talk to the doctors.

General Mmm?

James I said: I will talk to / the doctors.

General You promise me?

James Yes.

General Give me your hand then.

General stretches out his hand. James hesitates. At the same time Laela appears, holding a book and a plate of food. James warily puts his hand into the General's grasp.

And there's something else.

James It's too tight, Dad.

General There's something else.

James That's too tight.

General Something else you must / promise me.

James It's too fucking tight!

General releases him. Laela makes herself comfortable with book and food. She ignores the conversation that follows.

What?

General I want you to take Laela—mmm?

James I don't know what you mean.

General Take Laela—there she is—she's yours—take her. I'm giving her to you and I'm giving you both money— and money—listen—because I have arranged this—for the child. I want you to take Laela, and I want you to be my child's father.

James (*faint laugh*) To be your child's father.

General Those are my instructions.

James I'm not interested in your instructions, Dad.

General Not interested.

James No.

General (*puzzled*) You don't want Laela? Because Laela can make a man feel like a god. (*Slight pause.*) You should've seen her crouching under that tree. I said to her: what are you doing under this tree? She said: I'm fetching water. I said to her: well, excuse me you don't look as if you're fetching water, you look as if you're crouching under a tree. How is that fetching water?— where is your plastic container?—where is the spring? Oh, she said, I don't need a plastic container, I don't need to go to the spring. My father has told me that if I crouch here long enough, in the shade of these leaves, the water will come to me. (*Slight pause.*) I said: then you'll have a long wait, sweetheart. She said: oh no—the water is already here.

> *Slight pause.*

But now she won't even sleep under the same blanket. She thinks I'm a *mende*, don't you? *Unafikiri mimi ni mende.*

> *No reaction from Laela.*

(*Smiles.*) Cockroach. She thinks I'm a cockroach.

Jonathan Who thinks you're a cockroach, General? Not history, I hope. (*Grins.*)

> *Jonathan has appeared, mobile phone to his ear.*

(*into phone*) Yup, yup—I'm in the house—give me two or three minutes—okay?—no, no—keep them outside please—

> *As he speaks he shakes James's hand with warmth.*

Jamie—good to see you. (*into phone*)—What? I said keep them outside unless we need them—yup—yup—excellent.

*He ends the call and offers his hand to the General,
who simply stares.*

And how is the patient? Well rested after his many
labours? (*Slight pause.*) Getting enough fruit? (*Slight
pause.*) Because I have to say the reports pass through
my office—the medical reports land on my desk—in strict
confidence, naturally—and what I read in those reports,
General, is . . . well it's a story of almost super-human
endurance. (*Smiles.*) According to the doctors, this man
shouldn't really be alive at all—should he, Jamie? But
alive is what you are, and being alive have—well I'm
sure you know this—have certain—what?—obligations.
Obligations not only towards the living, but also—and in
your case very much so—obligations towards the dead.

Pause. The General continues to stare.

(*faint laugh*) You realise that's one big fucking African
headache you gave me?

Pause. The General continues to stare.

Big headache, General. Africa. Remember?

James He's not stupid.

Jonathan Not stupid—of course not—forgive me,
James—obviously not stupid, but very very dangerous:
a man, as I've explained to you, whose independent—and
I stress this—whose completely independent actions have
placed my government in a very delicate position. (*faint
laugh*) There were moments when I even started to
believe that indiscriminate murder—General—had been
my own policy. It was Kitty who kept me sane. The man
I love, she said, could never be responsible for such a
thing. Neither could the man I love be responsible—she
said—for protecting the person who is.

69

He takes a grape from the bowl of fruit, eats it, and smiles at the General.

'Crimes against humanity.'

General (*almost inaudible*) I killed the Nemean lion . . .

Jonathan What's that?

General I killed the Nemean lion.

Jonathan Uh-hu.

General . . . tore off its skin . . .

Jonathan Uh-hu. Very / probably.

General I killed the snake that guarded the tree . . . bore the weight of the earth . . .

Jonathan Uh-hu.

General . . . reached into the tree . . . broke into the garden . . .

Jonathan Uh-hu—very good.

General . . . killed the snake . . . reached into / the tree . . .

Jonathan (*beckoning*) Now I've brought someone with me, General . . .

General . . . reached into the apple tree . . .

Jonathan This is—I'm sorry: I've forgotten your / name.

Iolaos Iolaos—my name is Iolaos.

Jonathan This is—of course it is—Iolaos—

General . . . pulled the apples out of the tree . . .

Jonathan And Iolaos here has volunteered to make the arrest—d'you understand?—which I'd like him to do very calmly, and with the minimum—obviously—of / force.

General Arrest.

Jonathan Exactly.

Pause.

Iolaos Just need to fasten those wrists, General.

Housekeeper, Physiotherapist and Beautician have followed Iolaos into the room and watch. The General stares at him.

Forgive me, General, but I will have to fasten your wrists.

General (*trying to understand*) . . . 'to fasten your wrists' . . .

Iolaos Yes, sir.

Pause.

General And you are . . .?

Iolaos It's me, sir. Iolaos. I've volunteered to take you out to the vehicle. But first I need—I'm sorry but I really do need to fasten your / wrists.

General . . . 'to take me out to the vehicle' . . .

Iolaos That's right, sir.

Pause.

General (*smiles*) So you're a monkey.

Iolaos No, sir. I'm not a monkey. I'm Iolaos. I'm your friend. You saved my life.

General Saved your life? Oh? Why?

Jonathan Get him out of here / please. (*Puts mobile to ear.*)

Iolaos You saved my life. You ran into fire. You carried me—General—across the sand.

The General considers this, then slowly offers his hands to Iolaos who moves forward to fasten them.

Jonathan (*very soft, into mobile*) What?—no—keep them outside, keep them outside—just have the vehicle / ready.

General And are there cameras?

Iolaos (*to Jonathan*) Well?

Jonathan (*to Iolaos*) Mmm? (*Into mobile.*) One moment. (*To Iolaos.*) Sorry?

Iolaos And are there cameras?

Jonathan Of course there are cameras.

General Ask.

Jonathan What?

Iolaos Ask.

Jonathan (*into mobile*) Hello?—yup—listen: he wants to know if there are cameras . . . okay, okay . . . excellent . . . (*to General*) Yes, there are cameras—lots of cameras behind the steel fence—cameras / and lights.

General And the gods?

Jonathan (*to General*) What?

General And the gods? Will the gods be watching?

Iolaos The gods are always watching, General.

General Ask. (*Slight pause.*) ASK THEM.

Jonathan (*into mobile*) Okay . . . Now he wants to know . . . Listen: he wants to know about the gods—gods, the gods—yup yup yup yup, obviously. (*to General*) The gods will be watching: you have my word.

The General offers his wrists once more to Iolaos, who fastens them with a plastic strap.

General Then make it tight, Mister Monkey. That's not tight. Tighter. Make it cut.

Make it cut—good—in front of the cameras. Break open my body for the gods. Show me behind glass on television and I will explain on television how I have cleansed—how I have cleansed—how I have cleansed and purified the world. Tighter!

Jonathan (*softly into mobile during preceding speech*) He's been secured—yup—yup—have the vehicle ready . . .

Iolaos (*to James*) You.

General Tighter.

Iolaos Fetch him his jacket.

General Tighter.

Iolaos Fetch him his jacket—let's get this man / out of here.

General
And I will explain into the microphones
that my labours are at an end
that what I have done
is what I was instructed to do
and what I was instructed to do
was to extract terror like a tooth from its own
    stinking gums.

73

I will explain
from my own carefully prepared notes
and meticulous diaries
oh yes
oh yes

that I am not the criminal
but the sacrifice
not the criminal
but the sacrifice
not the criminal
but the sacrifice
not the criminal   **Jonathan** Come on, come
but the sacrifice   on: get him outside.
not the criminal
but the sacrifice   **Iolaos** This way, General . . .
not the criminal
but the sacrifice   **Jonathan** I don't want to
not the criminal   hear this. Just get him
but the sacrifice   outside.
not the criminal
but the sacrifice   **Iolaos** Come on, sir. Let's go
not the criminal   and find those cameras . . .
but the sacrifice
not the criminal   **Jonathan** (*softly into
but the sacrifice   mobile*) It's fine—yup—
not the criminal   yup—he's cooperating and
but the sacrifice   they're coming out now . . .

*The General is taken out by Iolaos, helped by the
three women. We hear their voices recede. Jonathan
remains in the room talking into mobile.*

(*off*) not the criminal
but the sacrifice
not the criminal
but the sacrifice
not the criminal
but the sacrifice
not the criminal
but the sacrifice
not the criminal
but the sacrifice

Their voices fade away . . .

Jonathan Okay, okay . . . Listen: tell them we are unable to comment for reasons of security but that a statement will be issued later.

Uh-hu, uh-hu—well I don't care who's asking—just tell them that the operation has been successful and that I will be making a full statement later in the afternoon.

Excellent, excellent.

The Boy appears. Jonathan ends the call. He seems about to speak, but changes his mind and goes out.

Only James, Laela and the boy are left in the room.

Laela reads aloud from her book.

Laela (*reads*) 'I wish I was not of this people. I wish I was dead or still unborn. We are the people. We are the people of iron. We work by day and in the night we grow sick and die. Our babies will be born with grey hair and god will destroy us. Father will not respect son and son will . . .'

James . . . despise his father.

Laela 'Son will despise his father and hurt his father with cruel words. The children of the people of iron will cheat their parents of what is owed to them, condemn them, and disobey their wishes.'

Faint music, growing in intensity.

'Men will turn the cities of other men to dust without reason. Shame and truth will put on white dresses and hiding their beauty from the people will abandon the earth.'

Laela continues to read, but is drowned out by the music.

Notes

19   *blue cards* Soldiers in combat carry blue or yellow cards which set out the rules of engagement.

32   *Tuseme club* 'Tuseme' is Swahili for 'speak out'. In central Africa Tuseme clubs are organised to empower girls and protect them from sexual abuse.

61   *call for fire* In combat, forward observers locate a target using global-positioning technology. They then 'call for fire' from the artillery.

64   *Kallinikos* 'Glorious victor.' Epithet traditionally applied to Herakles.

68   *Unafikiri mimi ni mende* Swahili for 'You think I'm a cockroach.'

70   *Iolaos* Friend of Herakles. When Herakles severed the heads of the Hydra, Iolaos cauterised the neck stumps to prevent the heads growing back.

71   *monkey* Military slang for military policemen, who are despised by the rest of the army.

75   '*I wish I was not of this people*' Laela reads from *Works and Days* by Hesiod, active c.700 BC.

77

FEWER EMERGENCIES

Face to the Wall, now part of the *Fewer Emergencies* trilogy, was first performed as a single play at the Royal Court Jerwood Theatre Downstairs, London, on 12 March 2002. The cast was as follows:

Gillian Hanna
Paul Higgins
Sophie Okonedo
Peter Wight

Director Katie Mitchell
Lighting Designer Paule Constable
Sound Designer Gareth Fry
Artistic Consultant Antoni Malinowski
Music Martin Crimp

Fewer Emergencies as a trilogy was first performed in its entirety at the Royal Court Jerwood Theatre Upstairs, London, on 8 September 2005. The cast was as follows:

Rachael Blake
Neil Dudgeon
Paul Hickey
Tanya Moodie

Director James Macdonald
Designer Tom Pye
Lighting Designer Martin Richman
Sound Designer Ian Dickinson
Music Mel Mercier
Costume Supervisor Jackie Orton
Company Voice Work Patsy Rodenburg

WHOLE BLUE SKY

Characters

2   She gets married very young, doesn't she.

3   Does what?

2   Gets married, gets married very young, and immediately realises——

3   Oh? That it's a mistake?

2   Immediately realises——yes——that it's a mistake.

3   She doesn't love him.

2   Oh yes, she loves him, she definitely loves him, but it's a mistake all the same.

3   Loving him makes it worse.

2   Makes it far far worse. Loving him makes it far far worse. What can she say? She can't say 'I don't love you'——it wouldn't be true. And at the same time what does she see?

3   Her whole life?

2   She sees——that's right——her whole life stretched out in front of her like a . . . hmm . . .

3   Corpse?

1   Corpse?——no——no——what?——no——that's not the way she thinks——it's more like a motorway at night——a band of concrete stretched out in front of her with reflective signs counting off the miles—— mile after mile after mile.

Pause.

She's not sure what to do.

3   Oh?

1   No——not at all sure what to do.

2   Leave him.

1   Well of course——yes——leave him——talk to
him very tenderly next to——well for example the
river——talk to him next to the river just where
the water swirls round the piers of the stone bridge.
Talk to him: patiently explain that she's made a
mistake——she loves him, but she's made a mistake.

2   She'll touch his cheek.

1   That's right: touch his cheek, ask him not to cry,
explain it's for the best, touch his cheek, take his
hand, comfort him——

3   As best she can.

1   Comfort him——obviously as best she can——
then get away. Pack and leave. Pick out just the
few books she really values, because what else does
she want?——all she wants is those few books and
to be free——pack the books and leave.

2   So she packs the books and leaves.

1   I'm sorry?

2   Packs the books.

3   Packs the books and leaves.

1   Ha.

3   What's funny?

1   Packs the books and leaves? No.

2   She gets pregnant.

1   She packs nothing. She says nothing. Not by the river, not in fact anywhere. She gets——and that's exactly what happens——gets pregnant——gets pregnant very young and has the baby. Look: there it is.

2   There it is screaming.

3   She can't love it.

1   Can't what?

3   Love it——can't love the baby——gets depressed.

1   Gets what?

3   Depressed——gets depressed——depressed by all that screaming——all that sucking——all that biting the breast.

1   Oh no. She loves it. She loves the child. She loves the way it sucks——even the way it bites. Loves its hair, loves its eyes.

2   Loving it makes it worse.

3   Oh? Makes what worse? The marriage?

2   Loving the baby makes the marriage worse.

1   Loving the baby *cements* the marriage.

2   Does what?

3   Cements it.

1   It cements the marriage. Yes. Oh yes. The three of them make a picture.

2   What kind of picture?

1   A picture of happiness.

2   What kind of picture of happiness?

1   What d'you mean: what kind of picture of happiness?

2   What does a picture of happiness look like?

1   It looks like them.

3   Oh?

1   It looks like the three of them——yes——in their winter hats. It looks like the three of them in the pet shop selecting a pet. It looks just how they look in the toy shop selecting a toy: pictures, pictures of happiness: that's what a picture of happiness looks like.

2   So she doesn't know.

1   Doesn't know what? What is there to know? She knows what the good schools are, she knows what TV programmes are or are not acceptable, she knows the importance of fruit, she knows what time of day the blackbird visits the garden and when the blackbird visits the garden she says 'Oh look: there's the blackbird visiting the garden.'

2   So she doesn't know.

1   Of course she knows——doesn't know what?

2   About the things he gets up to.

3   Oh? Does he get up to things?

2   Of course he gets / up to things.

1   Of course she knows——of course he gets up to things——she's not stupid——she knows what it means when his eyes slide away like that.

3   Oh? Under the winter hat?

1   She knows he gets up to things——yes, under the
     hat——even in the toy shop selecting a toy his eyes
     still slide away. She knows what's on his mind.

2   So she packs her books, takes the child and leaves.

1   Does what?

2   Packs her books——takes her child——leaves.

1   What books?

     Pause.

     What books?

2   The books.

3   The books she had at the beginning.

1   Did she have books at the beginning then?

3   Of course she had books at the beginning: student
     books.

1   (*smiles*) Oh *those*: student books.

3   That's right: the books she had at the beginning:
     student books.

1   (*smiles*) *Those* books——the difficult ones——the
     ones she had at the beginning——the ones she wrote
     her name in at the beginning——the books that
     made her feel alive at the beginning.

3   Yes: where are they now?

2   Good question.

3   What happened to those books?

2   Good question.

1   What happened to the books? Well the books are probably . . . hmm . . . somewhere in a plastic bag.

3   Oh?

1   Yes, in a . . . hmm in a plastic bag or something. Why?

2   So the books aren't part of the picture.

1   What picture?

2   The picture we were talking about: the picture of happiness.

1   (*smiles*) Oh *that*: the picture of happiness. You mean the picture of the boat: the two of them on the boat.

3   The boat? No. Not two of them on the boat, three of them in the pet shop, three of them buying the pet. What boat?

    Pause.

    What boat?

1   (*inward*) Ha.

3   What's funny?

1   (*inward*) That pet——that pet's so funny——the way it knows the difference between right and wrong—— the way it burrows when it's done right and when it's done wrong comes to the surface——comes to the surface——smiles at everyone——shows us its yellow teeth. And the name's so funny. What a funny thing for a pet to call its own child. What kind of name is that?

2   You mean for a child to call its own pet.

1   I said for a child to call its own pet.

2   You said for a pet to call its own child.

1   You think I don't know what I said?

3   Well we won't argue.

1   We won't argue because what I said was to call its own pet——what a funny thing for a child to call its / own pet.

2   So you're saying she's still there?

1   Still where?

2   She hasn't left the house?

1   Left? No. Why? Because of the things he gets up to? Why? No. Why should she? Look at the floors. Look at the walls. Look at the way the dining table extends and extends. On summer evenings it extends and extends right through the French doors and out under the Blue Atlas Cedar. Small lamps hang in the branches and everybody's laughing: the doctors and nurses, the butchers and the musicians who have become their friends: work friends, boating friends, friends from school——parents——traders and craftspeople with exceptionally rare skills——the very same people in fact who designed and built then polished with their own hands this ever-lengthening table where everybody sits under the blue tree and laughs in a boisterous but good-natured way—— I stress good-natured way——about all those things that make life worth living. Of course she's still there.

3   Of course she is.

1   Leave? Why should she?

2   What things are those?

93

1   She has no intention, thank you very much, of leaving.

2   What things are those?

1   What things are what?

2   Money? Property? Family?——The things that make life worth living.

1   (*smiles*) Oh *those*. Say that again.

2   Money? Property? Family? What is it?

3   Yes, what is it that makes the guests laugh so good-naturedly?

1   Why shouldn't they laugh?

3   I'm sorry?

1   Why shouldn't her guests laugh? Why shouldn't her guests enjoy themselves under the tree? Haven't they worked? Haven't they struggled to extend this table? Haven't they screamed at each other in private? Punched each other? Haven't they broken each other's skin to open this, for example, bottle of wine?

3   Oh?

2   Of course they have.

1   Of course they have.

2   Used the word bitch.

1   Used the word pig. Used the phrase——hmm . . . what's that phrase?

3   'Say that one more fucking time and I'll break your fucking neck'?

1   Used the phrase——exactly——'say that one more
fucking time to me and I'll break your fucking neck'
in order to hang the tree, for example, with these
tiny lamps.

2   You mean they have a right to laugh.

1   More than a right: they have a duty——just as when
they toast each other they have a duty to meet each
other's eyes.

3   I thought his eyes always slide away.

2   Not any more.

1   That's right: not any more. Now they stare back.
After these——hmm . . . what is it? . . .

She silently counts, using her fingers.

. . . eleven——after these eleven years of marriage his
grey eyes stare right back at hers.

2   Just as her grey eyes –

1   Exactly.

2   – stare right back –

1   Exactly——how did you know that?——into his.

3   'What is it you want, sweetheart?'

1 silently counts again on her fingers.

1   (*inward*) Or is it ten?

3   'What is it you want, sweetheart?'

1   (*looks up from counting*) What's that? I'm sorry?

2   She's asking him what he wants.

1   Asking who?

2   Asking Bobby.

1   Which Bobby?

3   Bobby her child.

1   (*smiles*) Oh *Bobby*——*that* Bobby——Bobby her child. Why? What does he want? Can't he sleep? What's wrong with him?

2   Maybe he'd like some fruit.

1   Maybe he'd like, yes, one of these plums. Or maybe he'd like just the tiniest sip of wine? No? What's that he's saying?

3   He's saying he can hear a noise.

1   What noise? That's just the guests laughing about all the things that make life worth living.

3   He's saying it's not the guests.

1   Not the guests? Then I'll tell you who it is: it must be Bobby.

3   He's saying no not Bobby.

1   Because Bobby is nocturnal. You know what nocturnal means. Nocturnal means that when you, Bobby, are asleep, that's when he——Bobby—— starts tunnelling.

3   He's saying no not Bobby.

1   Because what did we say to you?——we said to you: don't keep Bobby in your room——Bobby is very nice but Bobby is nocturnal——which means that when you, Bobby, are asleep, he——the Bobby you have insisted and insisted on keeping in your room——starts cleaning out his nest.

2   He's saying no not Bobby: it's a voice.

3   A voice? In the room?

2   In his head: he's saying it's a voice in his head.

1   (*smiles*) Well we all have those, sweetheart, we all
    have voices in our heads: those are our thoughts.
    That's when Mummy talks to Mummy: that's when
    Mummy says 'Where did I leave my hair-clips,
    Mummy?' and Mummy answers 'Well Mummy, I'm
    not sure: have you tried looking in the bathroom?'
    Or Mummy might say to Mummy 'Why when I
    smile does it always feel like I'm smiling in spite of
    myself? Why have I stopped feeling alive, Mummy,
    the way I used to feel alive at the beginning?' Or
    'Why——Mummy——has my hair begun to turn
    the colour of cigarette-ash?' So Mummy has to get
    quite tough with Mummy then. Mummy has to
    say things to Mummy like 'Pull yourself together,
    Mummy, and grow up' or things like 'Ten or eleven
    years of marriage don't make a woman any less
    desirable——'

3   Far from it.

1   Far from it——yes——'Any more than do a few
    flecks of grey.' These are our thoughts.

2   He's saying no not thoughts. He knows what
    thoughts are, but this is a voice. He says the voice
    doesn't like him. He wants you to come.

1   Of course the voice likes him. What does he mean?

2   He wants you to come. He wants you to sit with
    him.

1   Of course the voice likes him. Everybody likes him.
    What is it exactly this voice is saying, sweetheart?

3   Good question.

1   Well?

     Pause.

     Well?

2   He's saying the voice is too soft to make out.

1   Then how does he know it doesn't like him?

3   Good question.

1   Everybody likes him. Everybody has always liked
     him. Mummy——Daddy——people in shops——
     people in the street——people on market stalls have
     always offered Jimmy, for example a banana——bent
     down, hooked cherries / over his ears.

2   Offered Bobby.

1   What?

2   Have always offered Bobby, for example a banana
     ——bent down, hooked cherries / over his ears.

1   I said Bobby.

3   You said Jimmy.

1   Well whatever I said AND I KNOW FOR A FACT I SAID
     BOBBY people have always liked him: always offered
     him fruit, always offered him love, pulled down his
     winter hat to keep his / head snug.

2   He wants you to sit with him. He wants you / to
     sing.

1   Bought him pets, built him snowmen, assembled his
     jigsaws late at night so that in the morning he'd
     come down the spiral stairs to find the sky, and I
     mean the whole blue sky completed, cut the crusts
     off his sandwiches and taken / the cheese out.

2 He wants you to sing the / little song.

1 Clipped his fingernails——wants me to what?

2 To sing.

3 To sing the little song.

Pause.

1 (*cold*) Oh?

3 Yes.

1 Wants me to sing the little song.

3 Yes.

1 What does he mean?

2 Good question.

3 To blot out?

1 I'm sorry?

3 Is it to blot out?

2 Yes——good answer: maybe to blot out the voice?

1 What voice?

3 (*mocks*) 'What voice?'

1 (*smiles*) Oh *that*——the *voice*——well yes it may well be to 'blot out the voice' but listen——

3 Oh?

1 That song, the little song, that's . . . well . . . hmm . . . that's Mummy and Daddy's song.

3 Oh?

1 That is——yes, that is a private song.

3   Oh?

1   And don't keep saying oh like that because it is as
     you very well know a private song.

3   Oh?

2   A private song?

1   Yes it is Mummy and Daddy's private song and
     I don't want to hear you talk about it ever again.

3   Not ever again?

1   That's right.

2   Says who?

3   Says who? Says Mummy.

1   Is that understood: I don't want to hear you talk
     about it ever again.

2   In front of guests.

1   In front of guests. In front of anyone. Not tonight
     and not ever again.

2   Says who?

1   I'm sorry?

2   Says who: not tonight and not ever again.

3   Says who? Says Mummy.

1   Says what?

3   Says Mummy.

1   (*smiles*) Not says Mummy, sweetheart, not says
     Mummy: says the voice.

FACE TO THE WALL

Characters

Four actors are required
1 (male), 2, 3 *and* 4

Time
Blank

Place
Blank

/ indicates point of overlap in overlapping dialogue

1 Yes? says the receptionist, What can I do for you? How can I help you? Who did you want to see? Do you have an appointment?

2 He shoots her through the mouth.

1 He shoots her through the mouth and he goes down the corridor.

3 Quite quickly.

1 Goes——good——yes——quite quickly down the corridor——opens the first door he finds.

3 Walks straight in.

1 Walks straight in.

2 Yes? says the teacher, How can I help you?

1 Shoots him through the heart.

3 Shoots the teacher right through the heart.

1 The children don't understand——they don't immediately grasp what's going on——what's happened to their teacher?——they don't understand——nothing like this has ever / happened before.

3 Nothing like this has ever happened before——but they do understand——of course they understand—— they've seen this on TV——they've stayed up late as a special treat and they've seen this on TV——they know exactly what's going on and this is why they back away——instinctively back away.

1   Okay——so they back away——the worst thing they
    could do——back away——but they back away——
    they back away against the wall.

2   Against their pictures on the wall——'My house'.

3   'My cat'.

2   'Me and my cat'.

3   'My house', 'Me and my cat', 'Me in a tree', and it's
    interesting to see the way that some of them / hold
    hands.

1   And it's interesting to see the way that some of them
    hold hands——they instinctively hold hands——the
    way children do——the way a child does——if you
    reach for its hand as it walks next to you it will
    grasp your own——not like an adult who will flinch
    away——never touch an adult's hand like this or the
    adult will flinch away——unless it's someone who
    loves you——a loved one——anyone else will flinch
    away——but a loved one will take your hand like a
    child——they will trust you like a child——a loved
    one won't flinch away——a loved one will hold your
    hand because the hand reminds you of your love——
    whole afternoons for example spent simply feeling
    the spaces between each other's fingers——or
    looking into the loved one's eyes——the thick rings
    of colour in the loved one's eyes——which are like
    something——what is it?——don't help me——the
    precipitate——the precipitate in a test tube——but
    anyone else——an adult——will flinch away——just
    as the child——child A——now flinches away from
    what?——yes?

4   From the warm metal.

1   From the warm metal——thank you——of the gun.

Just as child A now flinches away from the warm metal of the gun. He shoots child A——in the head.

3   He moves on.

1   He moves on to child B. He shoots child B——in the head.

3   He moves on.

1   He moves on to child C. Child C——yes?

4   Tries to duck away.

1   What?

4   Child C tries / to duck away.

1   He shoots child B——in the head.

3   He moves on.

1   He moves on to child C. Child C tries to duck away. He shoots——no——yes——no——not shoots—— yes?

4   But to no avail.

1   Tries to duck away. But to no avail. He shoots child A——in the head.

3   He moves on.

1   He moves on to child B. He shoots child B——in the head.

3   He moves on.

1   He moves on to child C. Child C tries to duck away. But to no avail. But to no avail. He shoots child C——good——in the head.

2   And how's life treating him?

1   What?

2   Life——how's life treating him?

1   Life's treating him very well.

3   How's his job?

1   His job is fine——well paid and rewarding.

3   And his wife?

1   Is charming and tolerant.

2   And how are his children?

1   His children are fine.

3   How many does he have now?

1   Four. He has four and all four of them are fine.

2   What? All four of them are fine?

1   All four——yes——is this right?——are absolutely
    fine. He loves swinging them through the air and
    hearing them scream with joy. When he gets back to
    their beautiful house he picks them off the ground
    and swings them screaming through the air.

3   And how is his beautiful house?

1   Increasing in value daily——well constructed and
    well located——close to amenities——schools——
    shops——major roads leading directly to major
    airports——minor roads——no——yes——minor
    roads——yes——minor roads winding——is it?——
    don't help me——don't help me——yes——minor
    roads winding through meadows watered by springs
    welling up through the chalk.

3   And how are the schools in his neighbourhood?

1   The schools in his neighbourhood are fine.

3   And the shops?

2   Yes——how's the shopping?

1   Excellent shopping——excellent——yes?

4   And not just the big names.

1   And not just the big names. Excellent shopping——
    excellent——and not just the big names but——yes?

4   Those kinds of / smaller shops.

1   Excellent shopping——excellent——and not just the
    big names but those kinds of smaller shops you
    thought——not thought——imagined?——yes?

4   You thought had all but / disappeared.

1   Disappeared. Excellent shopping——excellent——
    and not just the big names but those kinds of smaller
    shops you thought had all but disappeared.

3   I thought those smaller shops had all but
    disappeared.

1   Well yes they have——but not here——not here——
    here you can find all those kinds of smaller shops
    you thought had all but disappeared. He moves on.

2   What? Artisans?

1   Artisans——yes——people who bind books——
    people who make shoes——people who grind
    knives——people who mend rugs——people who
    gut fish——cut cheese——people who mix paint.
    He moves on.

3   Medical supplies?

1   Medical supplies——catering supplies——motoring
    supplies——yes?

4   Spare parts / for cars.

1   Spare parts for cars no longer manufactured but lovingly restored. He moves on. He shoots child D——in the head.

2   So there must be blood.

1   Well of course there's blood——not just blood on the wall——not just blood on the floor.

3   But blood in the air.

2   Blood in the air. Blood hanging in the air. A mist.

3   An aerosol.

1   An aerosol——that's right——that's good——of blood——which he hadn't foreseen——he hadn't foreseen the aerosol of blood——or the sound——is this right?——this is right——or the sound of the distressed children when his head was on the white pillow——on the white pillow——don't help me—— when his head was on the white pillow picturing the scene——but now——don't help me——but now it's clear——now the picture is clear——and there's another sound——what's that other sound?—— don't help me, don't help me——the sound of his heart——no——yes——yes——the sound of his heart——the sound of his own heart——the sound of the killer's heart sounding in the killer's head—— that's right——that's good——which he hadn't foreseen——he hadn't foreseen the sound of his own heart in his own head——filling his head—— his own heart filling his head with blood——popping his ears——popping his ears with blood——like a swimmer——not swimmer——don't help me—— like a diver——this is right——diving into blood—— he's like a diver diving into blood——that's right——that's good——very good——down he goes——down he goes away from the light——

diving into blood——popping——popping his ears and what are you staring at?——eh?——eh?—— what are you staring at?——turn away——look away——no——turn away——that's right——turn away or you're next——be quiet or you're next—— that's right——that's good——you saw what happened to child A, you saw what happened to child B, you saw what happened to child C——you saw what happened to child C——you saw what happened to child C——no——yes——no——don't help me——

Pause.

Don't help me——

4   You saw what happened to child D.

1   Don't help me——you saw what happened to child A, you saw what happened to child B, you saw what happened to child C, you saw what happened to child D, so——so——you saw what happened to child D, so——

4   So shut the / fuck up.

1   YOU SAW WHAT HAPPENED TO CHILD D, SO SHUT THE FUCK UP. CUNT. CUNT. LITTLE CUNT. I SAID DON'T HELP ME.

Long pause.

3   So he's not a sympathetic character.

1   No.

3   We can't feel for him.

1   No.

3   Cry for him.

1   No.

3   He's never suffered.

1   No.

3   Experienced war.

1   No.

3   Experienced poverty.

1   No.

2   Torture.

1   Torture?

2   Been tortured——yes——for his beliefs. You heard what / I said.

1   No. What beliefs? No.

2   Abused, then, as a child.

1   No.

2   Fucked up the arse as a child.

1   No.

3   Or in the mouth.

1   No.

2   Beaten.

3   Beaten by his dad breaking a leg off the chair in the kitchen. Beaten with a chair-leg.

1   No.

2   What about his own children?

3   Yes——perhaps they're sick.

1   No.

2   His wife?

3   His wife what?

2   Sick?

1   No.

2   Is his car unreliable?

1   No.

2   What about the milkman?

3   Yes——is the milkman in his neighbourhood ever late?

1   No.

2   Or the postman?

1   Sometimes.

Pause.

3   How does he feel when the postman's late?

1   Angry.

2   So now he's going to kill the postman.

3   Typical.

1   Of course he's not going to kill the postman. It's not the postman's fault——he knows it's not the postman's fault——sometimes there are problems sorting the letters——the machine for sorting the letters has broken down, for example, and the letters have to be sorted by hand——or perhaps there are lots of parcels and every parcel means a conversation on the doorstep.

Pause.

A conversation on the doorstep——yes?

4   In the sunshine.

1   Means a conversation on the doorstep in the sunshine. And sometimes the postman's boy can't wake the postman up. 'Dad, dad', he says 'it's five o'clock'——

4   'Wake up. It's five o'clock.'

1   'Dad, dad,' he says, 'Wake up. It's five o'clock. I've brought you / your tea.'

4   'Time to get up.'

1   What?

4   'Time / to get up.'

1   'Dad, dad,' he says, 'Wake up. It's five o'clock. Time to get up. I've brought you your tea.' But the postman——don't help me——but the postman—— this is right——I'm right——don't help me——'Time to get up. I've brought you your tea.' But the postman——but the postman——but the postman just pushes himself harder against the wall.

*

Twelve-Bar Delivery Blues
Woke up this morning
Heard my son call
Turned away from the window
Turned my face to the wall.
Daddy daddy, he said to me
Daddy daddy, I've BROUGHT YOU YOUR TEA.

Son, I told him,
Your poor daddy's dead
There's another person
Come to live in his head.
Son son, your daddy's not well
Son son, your DADDY'S A SHELL.

There's another person
Speaking these lies
There's another person
Looking out through my eyes.
Son son, he's filing reports
Son son, he's PROMPTING MY THOUGHTS.

My son poured tea
From the brown china pot
Said, drink up your tea, dad,
Drink up while it's hot.
Daddy daddy, you're not sick at all
Daddy daddy, turn a-WAY FROM THE WALL.

Hey daddy,
You're a liar——and a fake
Take off those pyjamas
There's deliveries to make.
I lifted my head from my white pillow case
Threw my hot tea RIGHT IN HIS FACE.

Hey sonny,
If there's one thing I've learned
It's don't rub on butter
When your skin is all burned.
Son son, I ain't got no choice
Son son, I JUST HEAR THIS VOICE
(Saying . . .)

Doo ba ba-doo ba ba – Doo ba ba-doo ba ba –
Doo ba ba-doo ba ba – Doo ba ba-doo ba ba –
Doo ba ba-doo ba ba – Doo ba ba-doo ba ba –
Doo ba ba-doo ba ba – Doo ba ba-doo ba ba –
Doo ba ba-doo ba ba – Doo ba ba-doo ba ba –
Doo ba ba-doo ba ba – DOO DOO DOO DOO . . .

Woke up this morning
Heard my son call
Turned away from the window
Turned my face to the wall.
Son son, I hear what you say
But there just ain't gonna be no deliveries today . . .
(No way).

FEWER EMERGENCIES

Characters

Three actors are required
1, 2 *and* 3

Time
Blank

Place
Blank

/ indicates point of overlap in overlapping dialogue

Written 10 September 2001

2   And how are things going?

1   Well things are improving. Things are improving day by day.

2   What kind of things?

1   Well, the light. The light is improving day by day.

2   Getting brighter?

1   What?

2   Getting brighter? Getting brighter day by day? Improving day by day? Getting brighter?

1   What?

2   Getting brighter? Getting brighter day by day? Improving.

1   Oh yes. Yes. Improving, yes. Getting brighter, yes.

2   Good.

1   Getting so much brighter, yes.

2   Good. I'm pleased.

1   I'm happy you're pleased.

2   I'm pleased about the light.

1   I'm pleased about the light too.

3   We're all pleased about the light.

2   Well, yes, of course we are——and are they still boating?

1   Both of them are still boating.

3   What? Gliding past?

1   Both of them are still gliding past when they get the chance, and they get the chance more and more often. More and more often they get the boat out——they set sail——they glide past in the boat.

3   So things are improving.

1   They're improving day by day. Not just the light, but boating too. They get the boat out——they check the supplies——they test the satellite telephone——they leave the estuary——and before you know it they're out on the ocean——slicing through the waves—— travelling further and further afield.

3   More confidently.

1   Much more confidently.

2   How do they look?

1   Look?

3   Yes——good question——how do they look?

1   Well, confident——more confident.

3   You mean they're smiling? Or don't they need to smile?

2   They don't need to smile but they're smiling anyway.

3   What——in spite of themselves?

1   They're smiling——that's right——in spite of themselves. Or rather——no——correction——they know they're smiling——but equally they know the kind of smile they're smiling resembles the kind of smile you smile in spite of yourself.

3   Say that again.

1   I can't say that again, but what I can say is that they still sing that little song.

2   They don't.

1   They do.

2   They don't.

1   They do, they do, they still sing that little song like something you hear in the supermarket.

3   Or in the DIY superstore, or on the porno film——when the swollen cock on the porno film goes into the swollen cunt.

2   So things are looking up.

1   Things are definitely looking up——brighter light——more frequent boating——more confident smile——things are improving day by day——who ever would've guessed?

2   Mmm?

1   Who ever would've guessed? Who ever would've thought the two of them could set sail like that towards the world's rim?

3   World's what?

1   World's rim. The rim of the world. The edge.

2   What edge? There is no edge of the world.

1   Oh yes there is. Oh yes there is an edge of the world.

2   Well, we won't argue.

1   We won't argue because there is an edge of the world——it's as simple as that. There's a rim like the rim of a plate, and past the rim is——what?

3   We don't know.

1   We don't know——it's as simple as that——we don't know what's past the / rim of the world.

2   So how are things looking when they leave the house?

1   Things are looking great. Things are improving. The whole neighbourhood is improving. The trees are more established, they've kicked out the Mexicans, they've kicked out the Serbs, people are finally cleaning up their own dog-mess, nice families are moving in.

2   Italians and Greeks?

3   Greeks, Italians, nice Chinese.

1   Nice Somalis, nice Chinese, really nice Kurds, really nice families who clean up their own dog-mess and hoover the insides of their cars. And what's more they've identified the gene——no——correction—— they've identified the sequence——that's right—— of genes that make people leave burnt mattresses outside their homes and strangled their babies.

2   Oh?

1   Yes——strangled their babies and installed better street lighting. Things are looking up. It's taken time of course. They've aged. Their hair's gone grey. But it doesn't stop them being desirable——far from it.

3   It doesn't stop them being desirable——it doesn't stop them boating——it doesn't stop them heading, like now, for the rim of the world——far from it—— or installing cupboards——

2   Far from it.

1   Far from it. It doesn't stop them installing cupboards for Bobby at the top of the spiral stairs——

3   Cupboards of precious wood.

1   Cupboards——that's right——of precious wood installed by joiners for all of Bobby's things——all the things Bobby will need in life for pleasure and for emergencies.

2   Candles?

1   Well naturally there are candles, boxes of matches, fresh figs, generators and barrels of oil. But there's also a shelf full of oak trees, and another where pine forests border a mountain lake. If you press a concealed knob a secret drawer pops open——inside is the island of Manhattan. And if you pull the drawers out, spilling the bone-handled knives and chickens onto the floor, spilling out the chain-saws and the harpsichords, there at the back, in the dark space at the back, is the city of Paris with a cloth over it to keep the dust out. There's a wardrobe full of uranium and another full of cobalt. Bobby's suits are hanging over a Japanese golf course. His shoes share boxes with cooked prawns. On one little shelf there's a row of universities——good ones—— separated by restaurants where chefs are using the deep-fryers to melt gold and cast it into souvenir life-sized Parthenons. And hanging from the shelf, like the Beethoven quartets and fertility clinics, is the key, the key to use in emergencies, the key to get out of the house.

3   You mean he's locked in?

1   Well of course Jimmy's locked in——he's always locked in——he's locked in for his own protection.

125

2   Bobby.

1   What?

2   Bobby——not Jimmy——Bobby is locked in for his own protection.

1   I said Bobby.

2   You said Jimmy.

1   You think I don't know what I said?

2   Well we won't argue.

1   We won't argue because what I said was / Bobby.

3   What emergencies?

1   Oh, didn't I tell you?

3   What emergencies?

1   Oh, didn't I tell you? Because there's an emergency on right now. Rocks are being thrown——shots fired——that kind of stuff.

3   What? Cars are being overturned?

1   Cars are being——exactly——overturned and burnt.

2   Surely not Bobby's car?

1   Of course not Bobby's car——Bobby's not old enough to drive——but Bobby's neighbours' cars, Bobby's friends' cars, Bobby's parents' cars——yes——of course——are being first turned on their sides, then completely overturned, and burnt.

2   I thought things were improving.

1   Things *are* improving——less rocks are thrown—— less cars completely overturned——less shots fired—— there are fewer emergencies than there used to be—— but all the same, there's an emergency on right now.

It's on right now. And I'm sorry to say that one of those shots came through the kitchen window and caught poor Bobby in the hip.

2   Oh?

1   Yes——I'm afraid so——it caught poor Bobby in the hip which is why instead of running up those stairs, he's——what?

3   He's crawling?

1   He's crawling——that's right——that's good——up the spiral stairs. Using his arms mainly.

2   He wants to reach the key.

1   He wants to open the door.

2   He must be mad.

3   Open the door? He must be / completely mad.

1   Ah yes——but you have to know what's going on in Bobby's mind. In Bobby's mind, if he opens the door, if he lets people in, if he takes them up the stairs, shows them the cupboards of precious wood, the fresh figs, the knives and the uranium——if he lifts a corner of the cloth and gives them a glimpse of Paris——if he shows them the swollen cock going into the swollen cunt and lets them pick a restaurant or a string quartet——if, after a swim in the mountain lake, he lets them take home a human egg——then what?——they'll what?——they'll . . . Yes?

3   Love him.

2   They'll love him

1   Then they'll always love him.

Pause.

Exactly.

3   Ship to shore.

1   What?

3   Ship to shore. They're calling him from the boat. They're calling him from the rim of the world on the satellite telephone. 'Bobby? Are you there?'

2   He's not answering.

1   Well of course he's not answering. He's pulling himself up the spiral stairs. He wants to get / to the key.

3   'Pick up the phone, Bobby.'

1   He's got the hang of it now: pull with the arms—— let the legs drag——concentrate.

2   So things are looking up.

3   Things are definitely looking up——more efficient use of his arms——more understanding of the geometry of the stairs——improved / concentration.

1   Brighter light——more frequent boating——more confident smile——fewer / emergencies.

2   It doesn't worry them then?

1   What?

2   It doesn't worry them that Bobby's not answering.

1   Of course it worries them——that's why they smile——that's why they sing that little song.

2   They don't.

1   They do.

2   They don't.

1   They do, they do——they push their grey hair out of their bright grey eyes and sing that little song.

3   (*sings – very soft and relaxed scat-singing*)
     Doo doo-ba-dee doo doo doo ba-doo . . .
     Ba doo-ba-dee doo, ba doo-ba dee doo . . .

     *Say ten seconds of this. Then slight pause. Then the
     others join in in unison, singing longer and more
     intense phrases. The lights begin a slow fade,
     reaching black where indicated.*

1, 2, 3
     Doo doo-ba-dee doo doo doo ba-doo . . .
     Ba doo-ba-dee doo, ba doo-ba dee doo . . .
     Ba doo-ba doo doo doo-ba doo-ba dee doo . . .

     *Maybe twenty-five seconds of this. Then pause.
     Lights still fading.*

3   And Bobby?

1   Mmm?

3   And Bobby?

1   What he's losing in blood he's gaining in confidence.
     Light's flaring through the windows——flames——
     it's getting brighter——he can see the key——

     Black.

2   Things are improving.

1   Things are improving. He's further up the stairs. He's
     closer to the key. See how it spins——no——
     correction——swings——see how / it swings.

2   See how the key swings.

3   That's right, Bobby-boy. Watch the key. Watch the
     key swinging.

THE CITY

*Everything we do, in art and life,
is the imperfect copy of what we intended*

Fernando Pessoa
The Book of Disquiet

The City was first performed at the Schaubühne, Berlin, on 21 March 2008, in a German-language production. The cast was as follows:

Chris Jörg Hartmann
Clair Bettina Hoppe
Jenny Lea Draeger
Girl Helena Siegmund-Schultze

Director Thomas Ostermeier
Designer Jan Pappelbaum
Lighting Erich Sneider
Translator Marius von Mayenburg

The City had its English-language premiere at the Royal Court Jerwood Theatre Downstairs, London, on 24 April 2008. The cast was as follows:

Chris Benedict Cumberbatch
Clair Hattie Morahan
Jenny Amanda Hale
Girl Matilda Castrey/Ruby Douglas

Director Katie Mitchell
Designer Vicki Mortimer
Lighting Paule Constable
Sound Gareth Fry
Sound Associate Sean Ephgrave
Assistant Director Lyndsey Turner
Casting Director Amy Ball
Production Manager Paul Handley
Costume Supervisor Iona Kenrick

Characters

Clair
Christopher
both heading for forty

Jenny
heading for thirty

Girl
a small girl of what? nine or ten?

Time
Blank

Place
Blank

I

Clair holds a flat object in a plain paper bag.

After a while Chris comes on. He's wearing a suit, carries a case, has a security pass hanging from his neck.

Chris How was your day?

Clair My day was fine. Only—

Chris Oh?

Clair Only—yes—I was waiting on the station concourse this afternoon after my meeting—waiting for my train— when this man came up to me and said, have you seen a little girl about so high—I've lost her.

Chris Lost her?

Clair Well that's what I said. I said what d'you mean lost her?—what does she look like? He said, I've told you: she's about so high and she's wearing pink jeans. I said well in that case I've just seen her—she was heading for the taxi rank with a woman who looked like a nurse— I can't say for certain she was a nurse, but it looked as if she had a uniform on, under her coat. So then he says, why didn't you stop them?

Chris It wasn't your responsibility to stop them.

Clair Exactly. But of course that's not what I said—what I said to him was: well let's call the police. And that's when it turned out no no no it was nothing as serious as he'd led me to believe. Because the girl was his daughter, and the woman—who—I was right—is a nurse at a nearby hospital—the Middlesex—was his sister-in-law. The girl—because they'd just got off the train—the girl had been brought here to stay with the sister-in-law. But the man—the father—had decided at the last moment to buy his little girl a diary. So he'd gone into a shop to buy his little girl a diary. But when he came out with the diary, expecting his kiss, they'd gone.

Chris His kiss.

Clair Yes, to be kissed goodbye. I mean by his little girl. He said he didn't expect to be kissed goodbye by his sister-in-law because his sister-in-law despised him. Which is why—thinking about it—not me, I mean him, him thinking about it—maybe why the moment he was out of sight she'd deliberately dragged the little girl off.

Chris What? Was she being dragged?

Clair No—but they were moving quite fast. Maybe not fast for the nurse, but fast for the little girl.

Chris That's why you noticed the jeans.

Clair That's right.

Chris Because her legs were having to move quickly you mean to keep up with this woman, this nurse, this aunt dragging her to the taxi rank.

Clair Well no—I've said—not dragging—but yes—I certainly did notice the jeans.

Pause.

What about you?

Chris Mmm?

Clair How was your day?

Chris My day was good. Only my card wouldn't swipe. Took me fifteen minutes to get into my own building.

Clair Oh no. Why was that?

Chris Well I tapped on the glass and the only person in there was a cleaner so the cleaner came over to the glass and I held up my card and pointed, obviously, at my picture on the card, but the cleaner just shrugged—which is odd because I know all those cleaners really well.

Clair So what did you do?

Chris Buzzed the buzzer till somebody came. (*Slight pause.*) What's that?

Clair What's wrong?

Chris Wrong? Nothing. Why?

Clair It's just the way you said: 'What's that?'

Chris Nothing's wrong.

Clair Good.

Chris Nothing's wrong.

Clair Good. I'm pleased nothing's wrong. Because I wanted to show you this.

Chris What's that? The diary?

Clair He gave me the diary—yes. I said: you mustn't give me this—it's for your daughter. Because of course the idea had been for his little girl to write down all her thoughts and feelings about this big change in her life.

Chris What big change in her life?

Clair Leaving her father of course. Living with her aunt.

    Pause.

Have you not been / listening?

Chris Does it start in January?

Clair What?

Chris Does it start in January?

Clair Yes—it's just a normal diary.

Chris What're you going to do with it?

Clair I don't know.

Chris Write in it?

Clair I don't know.

Chris Write what?

Clair I've told you: I have / no idea.

Chris And he just *gave* it to you?

Clair Mmm?

Chris The man—this man—he just *gave* it to you?

Clair Well no—not right there—obviously—in the middle of Waterloo Station. He asked if he could talk to me. So because of what had happened—the little girl and so on—the fact I'd seen her heading off like that towards the taxis—I felt I didn't really have a choice. And I was glad, as it happened, because it turned out I knew him.

Chris You knew him?

Clair Yes—not knew him—but knew who he was.

Chris Oh?

Clair Yes. Well yes. He's this writer that everyone's talking about. Well not everyone—obviously—but people who know—people who know about writing. So of course that was completely fascinating—it was completely fascinating to find myself sitting in a café with this writer that everyone's talking about. Because he never gives interviews, but there he was sitting in this café opening his heart to me. About his time in prison—and the torture there—but all quite normally—just a normal conversation—just like me talking to you now—about torture—about the bucket on the cement floor—all quite normal—and the child of course—his little girl—the hopes he had for her—which made him sad—why is it, he said to me, that it's our hopes that make us sad—even there—in the dark—in the cell—which is why he tried not to—hope, I mean—I think I've got this right—during all the nights and days he waited for them to come—just waited and waited for them to come.

Chris Them?

Clair His torturers.

Chris I see.

Clair The people who were determined to / break his will.

Chris I had a visit from Bobby today.

Pause.

Clair Oh? Bobby Williams?

Chris Yes.

Clair What did Bobby Williams want?

Chris Just to say hello. Well—no—more in fact than to say hello. He came into my office because he wanted to tell me about this lunch he'd had with Jeanette. Because the week before last it seems he'd had this lunch with Jeanette and according to Jeanette the North American division is beginning to restructure and Jeanette's instinct is, is that if they're beginning to restructure in North America it won't be long before they start restructuring here.

Clair Oh?

Chris And of course he managed to make all this sound as if he cares about what happens to me and to my family but the truth is he wanted to see me squirm. And because of his relationship with Jeanette—which I would hesitate to call sexual—but because of this thing, whatever it is, this intimacy, these lunches they have—well because of that, Bobby's job is protected, whereas mine, given the situation in the North American territories, is, well is obviously much more vulnerable.

Clair Look: if the changes are going to be that radical, then even Jeanette won't be able to protect Bobby for the simple reason that Jeanette will be vulnerable herself.

Chris Yes, but Jeanette's very clever. I'm not saying she's indispensable—nobody's indispensable—but she's worked out a way of printing herself onto people's minds. I mean let's say, let's just say that this afternoon, instead of meeting this man at Waterloo Station, you'd met Jeanette, and that it was Jeanette who'd taken you to a café and told you this ridiculous story about the little girl and the nurse and about being tortured in a bucket or whatever it is this man tried to make you believe. Well in those two hours in the café—because I'm assuming you spent a good couple of hours with him—but in those two hours Jeanette would have made it her business to print herself onto your mind. You'd come away from that café, and regardless of her ridiculous story, or perhaps, who knows, because of it, you'd be thinking that Jeanette—and I've seen this happen—was essential to your company's survival. You'd be talking to me now—having, as you say, a normal conversation with me now—but in your head there'd be this current—this flow of speculation about Jeanette—Jeanette's grasp of the market—Jeanette's strategic vision—Jeanette's ability to think outside of the box blah blah blah. And once that flow started there would be no way you could ever dismiss her from your thoughts—the way for example you'll almost certainly dismiss this man.

Clair Oh?

Chris Yes.

Clair A flow of speculation.

Chris Yes. And you'd have no idea why. Because after all Jeanette is very ordinary-looking.

Clair Is she?

Chris And yet she has this power.

Clair Over men.

Chris Over what?—no—that's not at all what I mean—I mean over everyone—men and women / likewise.

Clair So you're saying you may lose your job?

Chris I'm just saying what Bobby told me Jeanette said to him at lunch. It doesn't mean I'm going to kill myself. I have no plans to hang myself from a tree, if that's what you think. There are, as you are well aware, two small children sleeping in this house, and I'm not going to leave them fatherless, any more than I'm prepared to let my decomposing body be found by someone out walking their dog. I hardly think I'm unemployable. And even someone who's spent a whole meeting with their head down drawing interlocking shapes on the agenda—or imaginary animals—will often come up to me afterwards and thank me for being the only person in the room to 've talked sense. Even Bobby Williams would grant me that. So I really don't think you need to be afraid.

Clair Afraid of what?

Chris Because obviously this kind of rumour is unsettling.

Clair I'm not afraid.

Chris Then why are you smiling?

Clair Am I?

Chris You know you're smiling.

Clair I had no idea I was smiling. (*Slight pause.*) Am I still smiling?

Chris You know you are.

Clair Then I must be smiling in spite of myself. Or perhaps I'm smiling because I'm looking at you in that suit of yours and remembering how much I love you. But—well—listen—what makes you think I've dismissed him from my thoughts?

Chris I'm sorry?

Clair Why do you call his story ridiculous? What makes you think I've dismissed Mohamed from my thoughts?

Chris Dismissed who?

Clair The writer. Mohamed. What makes you think I've dismissed him from my thoughts?

Chris Well haven't you?

Clair Yes—no—no—not necessarily.

> *Pause.*
>
> *He begins to laugh.*

What is it?

Chris You've stopped smiling.

Clair Have I?

Chris Yes.

Clair Really?

Chris Yes.

They both chuckle.

I'll tell you something that will make you laugh. You know this morning when I got to my building? Well my card wouldn't swipe. I tried and I tried but it *would not swipe.* So I tapped on the glass but the only person in there at that time of the morning was a cleaner so the cleaner came over to the glass . . . No. I've told you this. Have I already told you this?

Clair Go on.

Chris But I've already told you this.

Clair Told me what? Have you?

Chris About the cleaner coming over to the glass. About when I held up my card.

Clair Oh *that.*

Chris Well didn't I?

Clair Yes.

Chris So why did you say go on? (*Slight pause.*) Hmm.

Clair What is it?

Chris Nothing. Nothing at all. Where're you going?

Clair I'm going to put this somewhere safe.

Clair goes out with the diary. Chris remains. He does nothing.

*Clair works at a computer, referring to a book or
manuscript beside her.*

Chris appears—'casually' dressed.

*He stands behind her, watching her work. She takes no
notice. Time passes, then:*

Chris Don't you get bored with it?

Clair Mmm?

Chris Translating. Don't you get / bored with it?

Clair (*continuing to work*) Well of course I get bored
with it sometimes. Not everything people write is
interesting and even interesting writing—like this—can
be dull to translate. On the other hand, I do get to meet
authors, and some of them are real characters—they take
me out to dinner—introduce me to their families. Some
of them are much quieter. They're the crabs. As soon as
you pick up the stone they're hiding under, they scuttle
off to another one. D'you have to keep standing behind
me like that?

He doesn't move. She continues to work.

Chris So you're not ever tempted.

Clair Tempted to do what?

Chris To write something of your own.

Clair Me? (*Smiles, and turns to him for the first time.*)
What makes you say that?

146

He starts to walk away.

What makes you say that? Where are you going?

Chris It was the doorbell.

Clair What doorbell? I didn't hear it. Are you sure?

Chris I'm pretty sure I heard the doorbell.

He goes off.

She listens out for a moment and, hearing nothing, continues to work.

Finally he returns with a woman, Jenny, who is wearing a nurse's uniform under her coat. They are talking as they appear.

Chris Please. I'm sure you won't be disturbing her. She's just here—look—in the garden—working.

Jenny I don't want to disturb anyone.

Chris I really don't think she minds—do you?

Clair Minds what?

Chris This is—sorry.

Jenny Jenny.

Chris This is Jenny.

Jenny I'm Jenny. Hello.

Chris Can I get you something, Jenny—something to drink.

Jenny Oh no. I can't stop. (*To Clair.*) I just wondered if we could talk for a moment.

Clair I'd be very happy to. Let me just take these things back inside.

Chris I'll do that if you like.

Clair No. You stay here and talk to Jenny.

She gathers up her things and goes. Pause.

Chris So . . . you're a nurse.

Jenny Yes.

Chris Have you always been a nurse?

Jenny Yes.

Pause.

Chris I suppose a lot of nurses are men.

Jenny A lot of nurses—you're right—are men. But a surprising number of nurses—perhaps the majority of nurses in fact—are women.

Chris Is that so.

Jenny Oh yes.

Chris But you must be under a great deal of pressure.

Jenny We are all of us—yes—men and women—under an intense pressure. (*Pause.*) And sometimes the pressure is *so* intense . . . it's *so* intense that . . . (*She laughs.*) But this is such a beautiful garden. I can see it from my window. I often see your children running up and down shouting and screaming. I often think how extraordinary it is to see a garden like yours with children running up and down shouting and screaming—right here—right here in the middle of a city.

Chris Isn't our garden just like all the other gardens? Surely the city's full of this kind of garden—a patch of grass—a few plants round the edge we typically don't know the names of. I don't really understand what you're saying.

Jenny Of course there are similar gardens—but now I'm in your garden—right inside your garden—actually standing here—actually standing on this patch of grass—I realise that your garden genuinely is unique. We know each other, don't we. I've seen you somewhere—was it the opticians? Or I know what it is—looking in a freezer cabinet in the supermarket—digging right down into the packs of frozen vegetables—looking at the broccoli—digging right down—that was you—only you were wearing a suit—you must've been coming home from work.

Chris Yes.

Jenny Picking up some shopping on the way home from work.

Chris Yes.

Jenny And also—

Chris You're right.

Jenny I'm sure I've seen you—

Chris Oh?

Jenny Yes—standing at an upstairs window.

Chris You're right.

Jenny Because when you opened the door I thought to myself: I've seen that face before—in the supermarket or something—or standing at an upstairs window looking a bit sad.

Chris Can I take your coat?

Jenny What?

Chris Your coat.

Jenny Oh no. I can't stay. I'm working. (*Slight pause.*) I did want to talk to your wife, though.

Chris I'll call her.

Jenny No—please don't raise your voice. It frightens me.

Chris Well in that case I'll go and find her.

He goes. Jenny waits. She takes out a mirror and examines her face. The other two come back and watch her in silence. Then:

Clair You wanted to talk to me?

Jenny Yes.

Clair What about?

Jenny Mmm?

Clair What about?

Jenny You sound surprised that I want to talk to you, but the fact is we're neighbours, and even if your house is much bigger than my tiny flat, we still—or at least I imagine we do—still care about the same things: street lighting, one-way systems, noise levels and so on. Not only that, but we're both women—which means—well I hope it does—that unlike men we can hopefully define our territory without having to piss on it first.

Clair Do I know you?

Jenny I'm Jenny. I've told you who I am. We're neighbours. You've probably seen me getting into my car—or—like your husband over there—watched me in the mornings taking off my uniform when I've driven back totally exhausted from the hospital at a time when most people are getting up and listening to the radio while they have their breakfast. In fact I could probably fall asleep there and then, but what I like to do instead is

curl up in a chair with a nice piece of toast or a nice egg
and watch one of those old black-and-white films on TV.
Today for example there was the one where Humphrey
Bogart pretends to be in love with Audrey Hepburn but
ends up really loving her—really and truly loving her.
After that—well you've probably heard—I like to play
the piano for a bit. I'm not too bad at playing the
piano—I took it quite seriously as a child—and I always
warm up with scales and things like that—but the funny
thing is, is that although I can get all the notes and
understand just how intensely the composer must've
imagined it, there's no life to my playing. Emotionally
it's dead. Because you know what it's like when the sun
shines on the TV screen so the picture disappears and
all you see is the glass surface of it? Well that's what my
playing's like—hard and colourless. I'm not saying that
if you heard me in the street on a summer's day when
I had the windows open you wouldn't think 'Oh—
exquisite.' But if you stopped and began to listen—began
to really really listen—then the expression on your face
would turn—oh yes—believe me—to dread—the same
look I see on a patient's face when they're told that the
tumour growing in their lungs has now spread to the
brain—a kind of hardening—here—round the eyes—
because of course once that point's been reached then
death—well I'm sure you both know this—is inevitable.
But listen: I didn't come here to talk about my piano
playing.

Clair Oh?

Jenny Of course not.

Chris Then why have you—?

Jenny Yes?

Chris Then why have you—?

Jenny Yes? Come? Why have I come?

Chris Exactly.

Clair To talk to me.

Chris Mmm?

Clair To talk to me.

Jenny That's right.

Chris I'll take your coat.

Jenny No. Keep away.

Chris I'm sorry?

Jenny I said: keep away from me.

She smiles. Slight pause. To Clair:

Let me explain. I work hard. I get tired. I'm finding it difficult to sleep. My husband's gone to war. Not to kill. Of course not. He's a doctor. He has a gun—because all soldiers have guns—but you'd laugh if you saw the tiny tiny gun they give to doctors—no use at all for killing people—not the large numbers of people you have to kill in a war. It's a secret war. I can't tell you where it is, or I'd be putting lives at risk. But I *can* tell you that what they're doing now, in the secret war, is they're attacking a city—pulverising it, in fact—yes—turning this city—the squares, the shops, the parks, the leisure centres and the schools—turning the whole thing into a fine grey dust. Because—and I have my husband's word for this—everybody in that city has to be killed. Not by him. Of course not. He's a doctor. But all the same the city has to be pulverised so that the boys—our boys—can safely go in and kill the people who are left—the people, I mean, still clinging on to life. (*Slight pause.*) Because it's amazing how people can cling on to life—I'm a nurse—I see it

152

every day—I see people cling on to life almost every
day—and it's the same—according to my husband—in
this city: people in all sorts of unexpected places, clinging
on to life. So the boys—what the boys have to do is they
have to go in and kill the people clinging on to life. And
just to make things clear, they've got blue cards, and on
the cards, that's what it says: kill. And I know what
you're thinking: you're thinking it must be pretty easy to
kill people who are simply clinging on to life—any fool
could do that, you're thinking—it must be like—what?—
going round your house before you go away on holiday—
pulling the plugs out. But no—ah—well—no—because—
you see—and I have my husband's word for this—the
people clinging on to life are the most dangerous people
of all. (*Slight pause.*) Say you're one of the boys—and
you're patrolling a street and you notice an open hatch—
and the hatch leads to a drain—so you go into the
drain—you go into the drain because you think: hmm—
perhaps there's life in this drain—perhaps there are
people clinging on to life in this drain. And yes—listen—
sounds—scratching—sucking sounds—signs of life in the
dark—because it's pretty dark—of course it is—down
there—deep under the city—in the drain. So you drop
your goggles over your eyes and you can see—yes—
actually see—according to my husband— in the dark—
you can see the whole grey-green world of the drain
using your goggles in the dark. (*Slight pause.*) And yes—
look—here are the signs—here are the signs of people
clinging on to life: rags, blood, coffee cups—and the
stink of course—I'm a nurse—I smell it every day—the
particular stink people make when they're clinging and
clinging on to life. And there they are! 'Suddenly', like it
says in a book, there they are: a bright green woman
with a bright grey baby at her breast—right there at the
end of the drain—sucking—that was the sound you
heard—a woman giving suck. (*Slight pause.*) So the boy

thinks: (*without characterising*) 'Hmm, fuck this, fuck this you bitch. I can't just—well—kill. I can't kill a woman with a baby at her breast you cunt, you fucking bitch. Hmm, I know what I'll do: I'll get out my blue card and I'll check the rules, I'll see what it says about this, about mothers and their babies, in the rules.' So he reaches for his blue card to check the rules and that's when they're on him. Angry fuckers clinging to life in the drain. Angry and unscrupulous perpetrators of terror who'll stop at nothing to stay alive—use a mother and her baby simply to stay alive. A brick splits the soldier's skull. And the last thing the baby sees as its mother uses her finger to slip its mouth off her nipple is a serrated kitchen knife—and I have my husband's word for this—a small knife with a stainless serrated blade being used to cut the soldier's heart out—d'you see? (*Slight pause.*) I said: d'you see?

Clair Well . . .

Jenny Do you?

Clair Yes—of course—well no—see what?

Chris See what exactly?

Jenny I'm not talking to you. Keep out of it.

Clair See what, Jenny?

Jenny How difficult it is to sleep.

Clair Oh?

Jenny How difficult it is—yes—for me to sleep in the daytime with all this on my mind when your children are running up and down shouting and screaming. D'you see?

Clair (*faint laugh*) What—d'you want me to lock them indoors?

Jenny Would you?

Clair What?

Jenny Would you lock them indoors?

Clair Of course not. Of course we wouldn't lock our children indoors. Would we?

Chris Of course not.

Jenny Where are they now then?

Chris They're playing. They're playing in the playroom.

Clair That's right: they're playing in the playroom.

Jenny Locked in?

Clair No.

Jenny Locked in the playroom?

Clair No.

Slight pause. Clair and Chris exchange a glance and chuckle. Softly:

What makes you think we lock our children in the playroom, Jenny? The playroom doesn't even have a key.

Chris It doesn't have a lock, let alone a key.

Clair I think it has a lock.

Chris Does it?

Clair I think it does—yes—have a lock. But the point is—Jenny—

Chris I'll go and look.

Clair What?

Chris You've made me curious. I'll go and look.

He goes. Slight pause.

Clair (*lowering voice*) I'm afraid he's got like this since he lost his job. He's bored and he's always looking for things to do. That's why he wanted to take your coat. To feel useful. And when he brought it back to you, he wouldn't've just handed you the coat—oh no—he's started holding my coat up and expecting me to slip my arm gratefully into the sleeve, like some character out of those old films you talked about. (*Smiles.*) And of course being a man he makes them play these games—these horrible noisy games—makes them scream—shout out— shriek—tosses them into the air—pretends—I hate it— I can't watch—to drop them on their heads—when they'd rather—obviously—watch TV or a blackbird— well, wouldn't you?—building its nest. You're right, Jenny—we're women—we don't have to bang our fists on the table to make a point and the point you're making is a fair one. And the fact that summer's coming— obviously—makes it even worse. Because if you shut your windows, you won't be able to breathe, and if you open them—because I do understand this—even when the shouting and screaming stops—*if* it stops—instead of going to sleep, you'll lie there waiting and waiting for it to start again, even if it never does—a kind of torture, really. (*Smiles.*) I don't know what the solution is, Jenny. I can ask my husband—what—to cut his toenails—I can turn away my head if I don't want to be kissed (although of course that's more dangerous)—but what I can't do— Jenny—is ask him not to play with his own children—in the daytime—when he has no job—in his own garden.

Jenny What then?

Clair Mmm?

Jenny What can you do?

Clair There's nothing I can do. I'm very sorry.

Chris comes back, laughing.

Chris Incredible.

Clair What is?

Chris They *are* locked in.

Clair What d'you mean?

Chris You were right: there *is* a lock—they've locked themselves in—they've found a key.

Clair What key?

Chris Well they must've found one.

Clair What did you say to them?

Chris Well I told them to unlock the door immediately.

Jenny They've found a key?

Chris I can only think it was under the carpet. They must've pulled up the carpet and found a key—yes.

Jenny (*laughs*) Devils.

Chris Yes.

Clair What did you say to them?

Chris I've told you: I asked them to come out. I asked them what they thought they were playing at. I asked them if they realised just how dangerous it was to pull up a carpet and lock themselves in a room. Because now, I said to them, now, even if you get the door unlocked, there's no guarantee that you'll be able get the door open, because it will jam against the carpet. You'll be trapped, I said, you'll be trapped in that playroom, and if either of you has an accident in there—cuts yourself,

157

for example, and starts losing blood—then how will Mummy and Daddy be able to help you?

Slight pause.

Clair What did they say?

Chris Nothing.

Clair You're sure they're in there?

Chris Well of course they're in there. The door's locked.

Jenny She means maybe they've locked the door from the outside then run away.

Chris I know exactly what she means—I don't need you to explain to me what she means—but the fact is, is I heard their voices and if they haven't unlocked that door in another— (*Looks at watch.*) what shall we say?—forty-five seconds?—

He concentrates on his watch. The two women look at him. Ten seconds of this.

III

Chris exactly as he was, concentrating on his watch.
After ten seconds, Clair appears, in a light summer dress.

Clair You look funny. What're you doing?

Chris Mmm? (*Looks up.*)

Clair What're you doing?

Chris Funny?

Clair Yes. What're you doing?

Chris (*smiles*) You've been on that phone for over an hour.

Clair Have I? Sorry. I've been talking to one of my writers. He's inviting me to Lisbon. In October. Did you want to use the phone then?

Chris October.

Clair Yes—well—I say one of my writers, but it's the same writer—the one I met at the train station—Mohamed?—remember?—he'd lost his child? Anyway he's organising a conference—a conference about translation—and he's asked me to give a paper.

Chris Mohamed.

Clair Yes—don't you remember—last Christmas—he'd lost his little girl.

Slight pause.

Chris Won't it be hot?

Clair I like the heat. You mean in Lisbon?

Chris Yes.

Clair I like the heat. You know that. (*Slight pause.*) Is something funny?

Chris No.

Clair Then what does that look mean?

Chris It simply means I suddenly realise how much I love you.

Clair Oh?

Chris Yes.

Clair You suddenly realise?

Chris Yes.

Clair Fuck off.

Chris What?

Clair I said: fuck off. You're only saying you love me because you feel bad about yourself and you hope that saying you love me will make you feel like a better person than you really are.

Chris On the contrary: I'm saying I love you because I feel good about myself. I have some very good news.

Clair Oh?

Chris Yes.

Clair Is it about work?

Chris Yes.

Clair You've found a job.

Chris Yes. (*Slight pause.*) I've found a job. Aren't you happy for me?

Clair I'm very happy for you. (*Slight pause.*) What's wrong?

Chris Kiss me.

Clair No.

Chris Hold my hand.

Clair No—why?—not now. (*Slight pause.*) It's hot. (*Slight pause, smiles.*) Well anyway how did this happen?

Chris Won't you kiss me?

Clair Not now. Not when it's hot.

Chris I thought you liked the heat.

Clair What? I do like the heat. Of course I like the heat. But not being kissed in it, that's all.

Chris In which case I'm sorry.

Clair Don't apologise. Impose your will.

Chris What?

Clair Impose your will.

Slight pause.

Chris You mean force you to kiss me?

Clair (*laughs*) How could you force me to kiss you?

Chris I could come over to you. I could force you.

Clair Oh?

Chris Yes.

Clair How will you do that?

Chris I'll show you. I'll come over to you. I'll make you. It's simple.

Clair Is it?

Chris It's really very simple: I'll come over to you and I'll force you to kiss me.

Clair Go on then.

Chris If that's what you want.

Clair Go on then.

Chris Is that what you want?

Clair Why should I want that? What kind of woman would want that?

He doesn't move.

Jeanette?

Chris Who?

Clair Jeanette?

Slight pause.

Chris Is that what you want?

Clair It's no good asking me what I want, you have to impose your will. You have to impose your will or you'll be (*snaps fingers*) out, you'll be (*snaps fingers*) out of that plate-glass door before you've even arranged our photos on your desk. Because the world has changed—oh yes—and you'll have to be much stronger than this.

Chris I *am* much stronger than this.

Clair Then prove it.

A slight pause. He goes over to her. He touches her face, touches her hair. She doesn't react but she doesn't resist. At the last moment he goes to kiss her, but she twists her head violently away.

162

No! (*Smiles.*) And anyway how did this happen, how did all of this happen? How did you come to get this job or whatever it is—mmm?

Chris It's quite a long story, as a matter of fact. And I can't remember if I told you what happened at the end of last year but at the end of last year when the restructuring began, Jeanette got herself voted onto the board and the first thing she did in her new capacity as executive member was to quite unexpectedly force Bobby Williams—I think I told you this—to resign. And early in the New Year perhaps I didn't mention that Bobby was found dead in a hotel room in Paris where he'd told his family he was going for a job interview.

Well soon after the funeral in—hmm, when was that?—March?—I'd gone down to the supermarket one evening to buy meat and because I couldn't find the quantity of meat I wanted in the pre-packed section—I mean in the plastic boxes where they put the meat on the little absorbent mats—I had to go to the meat counter and there was something very familiar about the man behind the meat counter and it turned out we'd been at school together. I know—yes—incredible. I didn't know who *he* was, but he recognised me straight away, he said, 'I can see you don't remember me, but I know who *you* are, I recognised you straight away, you're Christopher, we went to the same school, it's the hat.' I said, 'How d'you mean—the hat?' He said, 'No one recognises me in this hat.' So he took off the hat—one of those white muslin trilby things they make them wear in the supermarket and I concentrated on his eyes and I realised there was in fact something really familiar about this person's eyes. So I said to him, 'Yes, you're right, I do remember you, but I'm sorry, even without the hat I don't remember your name.' So he goes, 'You don't have to remember it: my name's right here.' And what he meant of course was he

was wearing a name badge and on the badge was 'Sam'.
Of course. Sam. Sam from school. Jesus Christ. So I
asked him how things were going—how life was treating
him—which was really stupid because I could see that
life was treating him like shit: wearing a badge, dressed
in a stupid hat—but no—oh no—life was treating him
well, he said—the pay and conditions were well above
average—there was a friendly atmosphere and generous
discounts for staff—job security—good prospects—he'd
no complaints—what about myself? So I explained to
him that I was . . . well . . . what's the word . . . (*Bows
head.*) Hmm.

   Slight pause. Lifts head.

He's changed into this navy-blue tracksuit and we're
sitting in this pub and he buys me a drink and he says,
'You probably don't remember the day you spat on me—
spat all over my clothes—spat all over my face—cornered
me in the classroom with that friend of yours and spat
on me. You probably don't remember that, Christopher.
You probably don't remember spitting on my hair.
Cheers.' (*Bows head.*)

   Slight pause. Head still bowed.

We're sitting in the pub, we've had a few drinks, there's
me, there's Sam, and now there's Sam's friend Phil who
works in the warehouse, drives a fork-lift. Who's your
friend, says Phil. This, says Sam, is my old friend
Christopher from school, done very well for himself, lost
his job, arsehole, scuse my French. Oh, says Phil, sorry
to hear it mate, seen Indy? Not here yet? Maybe it's the
flight, says Sam, maybe there's fog, where's she coming
from? Abu Dhabi, says Phil, fucked if there's fog there,
what's she playing at? Give her a chance, says Sam,
beautiful girl like that.

Slight pause. Lifts head.

Okay—listen—I'm on my own—I'm in the pub—I've
had a few drinks—Indy walks in—I know it's her from
the logo on her jacket—the skirt—the works—the little
bag on wheels—Indy, I say to her, Phil's gone—I'm really
sorry but he wouldn't wait. Beg your pardon? says
Indy—who are you? where's Phil? what's going on? So
I try to explain—about the meat—about Sam from
school—his eyes—the white hat—treating him well—no
complaints—and she's looking at me—that's right— like
that—the way you're looking at me now—the same
disdain—this girl Indy—the same disdain—the way she
looks at the men in business class when they order
champagne—touch her arm and order champagne for
the girls they've left their wives for—silver-haired men
watching the rivers turn to threads—cities to maps—
whole oceans to a field of sparks—utter contempt—
yes—like that—like you—that look—BECAUSE WHAT
IS IT EXACTLY YOU'RE TRYING TO SAY TO ME?

Silence.

Clair Look. I'm just going to Lisbon for a few days.
It won't be till October. I don't despise you. Of course
I don't. And why should you care about the opinion of
a complete stranger in a pub? It's not as if you'll ever see
her again.

Chris No.

Clair Is it?

Chris No.

Clair Will you?

Chris No. (*Slight pause.*) Jesus Christ, no, I hope not.

Clair (*smiles*) Then stop thinking about it.

Chris I'm not thinking about it.

Clair Good—because you should stop thinking about it.

Chris Well I'm not.

Slight pause.

Clair I'm so happy for you.

Chris Oh?

Clair It's such wonderful news.

Chris Yes.

Clair You've changed completely.

Chris Yes. What? Have I?

Clair Yes, you've completely changed. You're much more . . .

Chris Am I?

Clair Of course you are.

Chris More what?

Clair More confident.

Chris Am I?

Clair Of course you are. Look at you.

Chris More confident.

Clair Yes. Look at you. Much more confident. You're a different man.

Slight pause: he bows his head.

Well don't you feel like a completely different man?

Chris Yes.

Clair Your whole attitude's changed.

Chris Yes.

Clair Even the way you're standing.

Chris Yes.

Pause. His head remains bowed.

Yes I suppose you're / right.

Clair Because let's face it: you've been impossible. You've stormed round this house shouting and slamming doors ever since Christmas. I close all the windows, but even then—well as you know, even then the neighbours turn up here complaining they can't sleep—and I can see them looking at the children, wondering if there are bruises under their dressing-up clothes. When I've tried to work you've sat at the other end of the table writing shopping lists, or stood behind me, criticising my choice of words. You've almost stopped being interested in sex—and when you have been interested, it's felt like a business opportunity, or a bank loan—forgive me—arranged over the phone. But now—

Chris Yes.

Clair But now—

Chris You're right.

Clair But now—

Chris Now what?

Clair Because I'd been dreading summer, but now your whole attitude's changed.

Chris Even the way I'm standing.

Clair Yes.

Chris Even the way the trees look. Even the roses have changed.

Clair Yes. Even the forget-me-nots.

Chris You know what we ought to do.

Clair What's that?

Chris We ought to celebrate. We ought to all get in the car and celebrate. We ought to all drive up the motorway into the oncoming traffic and celebrate. Don't you think? Or I know what: invite someone round.

Clair Who?

Chris People—people we know—friends. Bobby for example.

Clair What d'you mean: Bobby?

Chris Bobby—Bobby Williams—invite him round to celebrate—eh? Get him to bring Jeanette.

Slight pause.

Clair (*laughs*) I don't think that's funny.

Chris He's a friend. He's someone we know.

Clair (*laughs*) Stop it.

Chris Because there are a number of things, sweetheart, I don't quite understand—and some of them are things I'll never understand—and I'm quite happy for there to be some things I'll never understand—but one of the things I don't understand but that I really would like to understand is why you say that it's hot. Because—well—what with the trees and so on—what with the shade and the air—because I can feel it—moving through the house—see what I mean? (*Slight pause.*) You see what I mean about the heat? You see what I mean about not wanting to be kissed?

Clair (*laughs*) Who doesn't want to be kissed?

Chris You don't.

Clair (*laughs*) What makes you say that?

Chris Well do you?

Clair (*laughs*) What? Want to be kissed?

Chris Do you?

Clair It's no good *asking*.

Chris Mmm?

Clair It's no good *asking* me. (*Slight pause.*) It's no good asking a woman if she wants / to be kissed.

Chris Well shall I assume that you do, then? Shall I come over to you? Shall I assume—mmm?—that that's what you want? (*Slight pause.*) Listen: I'm going to assume that that's what you want.

Clair Go on then.

Chris I'm going—you're right—to impose my will.

Clair Go on then.

   He doesn't move. Slight pause.

Chris Are you crying? Why are you crying? Don't cry. Why are you crying?

Clair BECAUSE I AM ANGRY.

   On this line, music in the distance from Jenny's flat: Schubert, 'Moments Musicaux', No. 3 in F minor. Pause. The music plays.

Chris I don't understand. You were laughing. Just a moment ago you were laughing (*Slight pause.*) Bruises? Why did you say that? Why would anyone think we'd harm our children? We love our children—love's what brought them into the world. Well didn't it—didn't it?

Pause. Music continues.

You're being unreasonable.

Clair (*wiping her eyes*) Where're you going?

Chris I'm going to watch TV.

Clair I thought you wanted to celebrate.

Chris I'm going to hoover then I'm going to watch TV.

Clair But you haven't even told me what the job is.

He looks back at her for a moment, then goes, leaving her alone. A few more seconds and the piece of music, which has begun in the minor, comes to an end in the major.

IV

Chris is listening to a girl of what? 9 or 10? reciting poems. The girl wears a coat over a nurse's uniform, exactly like Jenny in Scene ii.

On stage is a concert grand piano, with the lid closed.

Pause.

Chris (*smiles*) Go on.

Girl
There once was a pianist called Jo
Who played every piece far too slow.
    When she got to the end
    She would turn to a friend
And say: 'You don't have to tell me. I know.'

Pause.

Chris Go on.

Girl
There once was a girl called Jo Gupta
Who slept with a famous conductor.
    But her friends were naive
    And just wouldn't believe
A famous conductor had fucked her.

Pause.

Chris Go on.

Girl
There once was a child in a drain
Who longed for the sound of the rain.

But when the storm broke
The poor child awoke
In a stream of unbearable pain.

Slight pause. Chris chuckles. Girl smiles.

Chris Who taught you that?

Girl Mummy did.

Slight pause.

Chris Take off your coat, sweetheart. You look hot. You can't play the piano with your coat on.

Girl I'm not going to play the piano.

Chris Yes you are. You're going to let me hear the piece you're going to play Mummy when she comes home. Take off your coat. Come on.

She unbuttons her coat. He takes it and holds it. Her uniform, though tiny, is not a 'play' uniform but a precise copy of that worn by Jenny.

How are those patients today? How's Charlie?

Girl Charlie's lost a lot of blood.

Chris I hope not.

Girl Now he's on a drip.

Chris I hope it's not all over the playroom carpet, sweetheart, like it was last time. (*Slight pause.*) Why are you wearing a coat anyway?

Girl We were outside.

Chris Oh?

Girl Yes, we were watching a blackbird build its nest.

Chris That's nice.

Girl It sang to us.

Chris That's very nice, only I don't think you were watching a blackbird build its nest. I don't think blackbirds make nests—sweetheart—in October. I think they perch on TV aerials—I think they hop across the grass keeping their legs together and stand suddenly very still, with their heads tipped to the side—but I don't think they make nests.

Girl We saw it. We both saw it. It had moss in its beak.

Chris Then how did it sing? (*Slight pause.*) October is when the leaves change colour, not when birds build their nests—mmm? Aren't you collecting pretty leaves at school? Aren't you getting out nice bright paints and printing leaf-shapes onto sheets of white paper? Eh? (*Smiles.*) Aren't your teachers explaining about the seasons? Haven't they told you how the earth leans away from the sun? (*Slight pause.*) What about conkers? When I was your age my coat pockets were full of them—but yours—well . . .

> *He's still holding her coat. He reaches towards one of the pockets. She makes a tiny move as if to stop him, then checks herself. He notices this, meets her eyes for a moment, smiles, then pushes his hand into the pocket.*

What's this, sweetheart? What's this in your pocket?

> *He withdraws his hand: there's a red sticky substance on his fingers. He lifts his fingers to his nose and sniffs—or perhaps tastes.*

Girl It was Charlie.

Chris What was Charlie?

Girl The blood. It was Charlie.

Chris It's no good blaming Charlie. Charlie is too small.

Girl He's not too small to be bad. You should punish him.

Chris He's not bad.

Girl Hit him.

Chris Don't talk like that.

Girl Punish him. Hit him.

Chris Hey hey hey—I said I don't want to hear you talk like that. Understood?

He wipes his fingers on the coat and drops the coat on the ground.

Let me hear your piece, sweetheart.

Girl And he opens doors.

Chris Does what?

Girl He *is* bad. He opens doors. He found Mummy's writing.

Chris You mean her work. Well I hope you've made it tidy.

Girl Not work—writing. She's been writing in a secret diary. He opened her wardrobe and he found a secret diary under her shoes.

Slight pause.

Chris Well I hope you haven't been reading it.

Girl Charlie can't read.

Chris I'm not talking about Charlie. (*Slight pause.*) You do know that it's wrong to read somebody's secret diary. (*Slight pause.*) Think how you'd feel if somebody read your secret diary.

Girl If I had a secret diary no one would ever find it.

Chris But what if they *did* find it? What if they read your secret thoughts.

Girl I don't have any secret thoughts. (*Slight pause.*) I want my coat.

Chris Mmm?

Girl I want my coat back.

Chris Your coat is dirty, sweetheart. Look at it.

Girl I want it back. I'm cold.

Chris You can't be cold. You're indoors. It's October and the heating's on. (*Slight pause.*) Look, if I let you wear your coat, will you play your piece for Mummy when she wakes up?

Girl Mummy's not here. Mummy's at a conference.

Chris Will you?

Girl Mummy's not here.

The girl hesitates, then takes a step towards the coat.

Chris (*stopping her verbally.*) Uh-uh. (*Smiles.*)

He picks up the coat himself and holds it up for her to put on. She comes over, tries to get her arm in the sleeve, but gets in a muddle.

(*Smiles.*) Wrong arm, sweetheart.

They try again and again get in a muddle.

Girl I can't get my arm in.

Chris What's wrong?

Girl I can't get my arm in the right place.

Chris What?—come on—you're / not trying.

Girl I can't get my arm into the sleeve. It's the way you're / holding it.

Chris Alright, alright, just do it yourself. JUST DO THE FUCKING THING YOURSELF.

He moves away, turns his back. The girl calmly puts on the coat and calmly buttons it. Then:

Girl Daddy?

Chris What?

Girl Shall I play you my piece now?

Chris (*begins very soft and fast*) Listen, sweetheart, there's something you ought to know: Mummy came home last night—she came home from Lisbon in the middle of the night—well—like it says in a book— 'unexpectedly'—and went straight to bed. She's here now—yes—that's right—in the house—but I've left her asleep because she was so tired. (*Laughs.*) You should've seen her. She was so worn out that she didn't even go into your room, she didn't even have the strength (she said) to push the hair back behind your ear and kiss you, the way she normally does. Not because she was unhappy—you're not to think that Mummy was unhappy—because—well—in fact she was laughing. That's how I knew she was home. I heard Mummy laughing out in the street—and there she was—under the street-lamp—sharing a joke—something about crocodiles—with the taxi driver out in the street. (*Laughs.*) Oh, it was windy! You should've seen all the leaves swirling round the shiny black taxi under the orange light. And when she came through the front door—still laughing, by the way—guess what: two enormous chestnut leaves followed her right into the house. (*Laughs.*)

I said 'Well this is a surprise: I didn't expect you back till the middle of next week!'

Girl And what did Mummy say to that?

Chris Mmm?

Girl And what did Mummy say to that?

Chris I've told you, sweetheart: Mummy was tired—she didn't say anything.

Girl Not even when the leaves came in?

Chris What leaves?

Girl You said two enormous leaves came into the house.

Chris Well yes they did—two enormous leaves *did* come into the house—but Mummy didn't even see them, sweetheart, because of the way she was clinging on to me.

Girl Was she afraid?

Chris (*laughs*) Of course she wasn't afraid. It wasn't that kind of clinging.

Girl Maybe she was afraid that someone would find her secret diary, and that's why she came back home.

Slight pause. In the distance an alarm clock starts ringing.

Chris Why don't you run off and play.

Girl That's Mummy's clock.

Chris I know it's Mummy's clock—and that's why I want you to run off and play.

Girl I want to see her.

Chris You can see her after we've talked.

Girl What are you going to talk about?

Chris We won't know, sweetheart, what we're going to talk about until we start talking. Now off you go.

Girl The diary?

Chris Of course not the diary. The diary—remember?— is a secret. Kiss?

He bends down. She kisses his cheek.

Good girl.

Girl What about the piano?

Chris The piano can wait. Now off you go.

The girl runs off. The alarm clock gets louder and after a few moments Clair appears, holding the clock, which is still ringing. She puts it down on the piano, which makes the sound even louder, and watches it until the ringing stops.

Clair (*turns to him*) Thank you.

Chris Oh?

Clair Thank you—yes—for letting me sleep.

Slight pause.

Chris So how was your conference?

Clair Mmm?

Chris The conference—in Lisbon—how was it?

Clair Oh it was a marvellous conference. People from all over the world converged on Lisbon to talk about books. Can you imagine? Authors read passages from their books and talked about what had inspired them. And the translators talked about the authors and how hard it was to translate the authors and the authors spoke very highly of the translators and were even, some of them, translators themselves, which meant that they had interesting things to say not just about writing but about translating too. And after lunch we'd all go off into little rooms—split up I mean—and go off into little rooms—those funny little rooms they have in Lisbon—take some particular topic—poetry—politics—and really pull it apart—really examine poetry or politics under the knife—put these things really and truly under the knife—just five or six of us in a little room really concentrating—I can't explain what it was like.

Chris You've just told me what it was like.

Clair (*smiles*) No. Because it wasn't like that at all, you see.

   Pause.

And my paper went well.

Chris Good.

Clair Went really well. My hand shook at the beginning, but everybody paid attention—even laughed at my jokes.

Chris You? Jokes?

Clair Yes—because I was nervous—obviously—about the jokes—but the jokes worked.

Chris What jokes? Tell me one.

Clair What?

Chris Tell me a joke.

Clair Not that kind of joke—not a joke you 'tell'—just ways of putting things—phrasing things—and Mohamed was pleased—he came up to me afterwards—in fact he sought me out—

Chris Oh?

Clair Yes—sought me out—singled me out I mean in the cafeteria and in front of everyone he knocked me into a table.

Chris Hurt you?

Clair No no—just rushed over to thank me and knocked me backwards into a table. He was so clumsy—this big bear of a man knocking me off my feet—I couldn't help smiling to myself.

Chris Like you are now?

Clair What?

Chris Like you are now—smiling to yourself like you are now?

Clair Of course I'm not smiling to myself. I'm smiling at you.

Chris Oh? Are you? Why?

Clair Of course I'm smiling at you. You're my husband. You're my husband, and— What're you doing?

Chris Sorry?

Clair You backed away.

Chris I did what?

Clair You backed away.

Chris No.

Clair I stepped towards you and you backed away. You know you did. (*Slight pause.*) Why did you back away from me?

    Pause.

Look. I'm here. I'm home. What more do you want from me? Try to understand. I open my door and what do I see? A man I very much respect. He wants to talk. He says he has a confession to make. What d'you mean, Mohamed, I say, a confession, can't it wait. No, it can't wait, he has to talk to me now, right now. Alright, Mohamed, let's go downstairs, I say, let's go down to the bar together, let's talk there. I can't, says Mohamed, I can't say what I have to say to you in the bar. So— look—I'm not stupid—I tell Mohamed that in that case he'll have to wait till morning because it's late, I'm tired, and I want to go to bed. No, says Mohamed, I have to come in, you have to let me talk, there's something I need to confess, don't close the door. So what can I do? D'you see? Mmm? Try to understand. Because this is a man that I very much respect—because of what he's suffered— and written about. So I let him into my room and he sits down in front of the window which I've kept open because of the heat and he says to me my child is dead. I say what d'you mean Mohamed, your child is dead? He says she's been knocked over by a car, she's dead, I just had a call from my sister-in-law. You mean the little girl I saw at the station? Yes, he says—Laela—she was crossing the road to post a letter. And he just sits there in front of the window looking down at his hands.

Slight pause.

Chris Waiting for you to comfort him.

Clair What?

Chris He was waiting for you to / comfort him.

Clair Well obviously—yes—I thought—of course I did— thought about going to him—putting my arm around him—thought about attempting to comfort him. But that's when he looked up at me. He looked up at me and what was strange was that his eyes—which were grey— had always been grey—were grey at the station—were

grey in the cafeteria—his eyes had turned—and I don't
mean the light—I mean the eyes themselves—had turned
black. His eyes had turned black like the inside of a
poppy and he said to me, I still haven't confessed. I said,
look Mohamed, you're upset, you don't need to confess,
you need to go to your sister-in-law, you need to try and
sleep, let's see if there's a pharmacy still open. He said to
me, no no no I still haven't confessed. And this time he
frightened me.

Chris You should've asked him to leave.

Clair Of course, but how? I said, you've got nothing to
confess, Mohamed, it was an accident. Oh yes, he said, it
was an accident, but listen Clair, what you have to know,
and what I didn't tell you when we first met, is why
I sent my little girl away. I sent her away because she got
under my feet, because she stopped me writing, because
she constantly interrupted my work, and sometimes,
when I shouted at her, because she had interrupted my
work, to ask for a drink, or to be read a story, her small
body jerked back, he said, as if hit by a bullet. Me, he
said, a writer, refusing my own child a story. Come on,
Mohamed, I said, come on, we all get angry with our
children, it's normal. No, said Mohamed, nothing a
writer does is normal, and besides that's not what I'm
confessing, because that is, as you say, something that
is entirely human and banal. No, what I have to tell you
is that the moment I finished speaking to my sister-in-law
tonight, and put down the phone, I experienced—and
the nearest thing to the word he used is 'exaltation'—I
experienced a secret exaltation, he said, as I realised that
what had happened could only enhance my work. My
child, you see, is like a log thrown into the fire, making
the fire burn, he said, more brightly.

Pause.

Chris Thrown into the fire.

Clair That's what he said—yes—like a piece of wood.
So I was very angry then—with Mohamed. I told him
I didn't care how many people he'd killed in his never-
ending fight for freedom and democracy, or how many
days he'd been tortured or how many prizes he'd won
for describing it. I told him I was disgusted by what he
called his exhilaration or his exaltation or whatever the
fuck it was and I wanted him out—I wanted him to GET
OUT OF MY ROOM.

Chris And did he?

Clair I'm sorry?

Chris Did he get out of your room?

Pause. She looks away.

So you believed him.

Clair Yes. No. Of course I did. Believed what?

Chris That his child was dead.

Clair Laela. Yes. He told me.

Chris So she won't be needing the diary then.

Pause. She meets his eyes. He smiles at her.

V

Jenny alone, wearing pink jeans and high-heeled shoes. She takes out a mirror and inspects her face. She puts away the mirror. She looks at the piano, whose lid is now up. She runs her fingers over the keyboard without making any sound.

Clair enters.

Jenny It's very nice here. I had no idea—to be honest—it would be so nice inside your house. It's warm—and surprisingly peaceful. You have such lovely things, like this piano. And I've just realised that now the leaves have gone, I can see my own windows. (*Slight pause.*) Oh—and this is for you.

> *She hands Clair a small parcel, which Clair begins to unwrap.*

Clair You're right. It's a nice house. It's warm in every sense. We're very happy here.

> *Pause.*

Jenny How're your children?

Clair Mmm?

Jenny How're your children?

Clair They're not bothering you, are they?

Jenny What?

Clair I said: they're not bothering you—not keeping you awake.

Jenny Oh no. I don't hear them. Or if I do it makes me feel . . . well . . . Hmm.

Clair finishes unwrapping the present: a small serrated kitchen knife.

(*Smiles.*) I hope you like it. I thought it would be useful with small children.

Clair Oh?

Jenny To cut up their food.

Clair You're right. (*Goes to kiss her.*) Thank you.

Jenny Careful! (*Steps back.*)

Clair Mmm?

Jenny The knife.

Clair Of course. Sorry. (*Points the knife away or puts it down.*) Thank you, Jenny. (*Kisses her.*)

Slight pause.

Jenny I haven't seen your children.

Clair Oh they're probably racing up and down excitedly on their new bikes.

Jenny What, with your husband?

Clair Mmm?

Jenny With your husband?

Clair Oh no—my husband found a job—he's working.

Jenny What? At Christmas?

Clair You sound surprised, but surely it's not unusual. It's not just doctors and soldiers, it's not just nurses like yourself, Jenny, who work at Christmas-time. Commerce can't stop any more than the course—isn't this right?—

of some fatal diseases. And while you and I are sitting in front of the fire like this,* unwrapping our gifts, people still need to buy things.

Pause.

What's wrong?

Jenny I don't know. Nothing feels right. Everything—don't you think?—seems awkward and artificial. I put these shoes on specially—but I'm not really comfortable in them—and if I'm honest, I don't know why I'm wearing them. Even a normal conversation like this—with a person I like—because I certainly like you—don't get me wrong—but even this—I don't know why—seems strained. I don't really know why I'm here at all.

Clair (*smiles*) You're here, Jenny, because I invited you. And if your shoes feel uncomfortable—well—simple—take them off.

Jenny You say your children are out on their bikes—but I can't hear them—I didn't see one single child when I walked here from my flat—nobody was out—it was so quiet—it was unnatural.

Clair Christmas is always like that: everyone's indoors with their families.

Jenny It didn't feel right. There were no smells in the air. People had wreaths on their front doors, but I couldn't see anybody through the windows, even though they had lights flashing round the window frames. And before I came out, I spoke to my husband and he just sounded angry.

Clair Maybe he misses you.

* *There is no fire. They are not sitting.*

Jenny Well that's not my fault.

Christopher enters. He wears the outfit of a supermarket butcher's assistant: a white hat with a brim, a white smock, and pinned to the smock a badge with his name: 'Chris'.

Chris (*kisses Clair on the cheek*) Hello sweetheart. We have a guest.

Clair This is Jenny.

Chris Jenny. Of course. Hello.

Clair How was work?

Chris Totally mad. Sam's off sick and Janine can't tell a pig's ear from a cow's arsehole, scuse my French. (*Chuckles.*) But listen: we know each other.

Jenny Yes.

Chris Don't we.

Jenny Yes.

Chris Wednesdays.

Jenny That's right.

Chris Wednesday afternoons: minced steak—two hundred grams.

Jenny Yes.

Chris I find myself asking: who is it who's eating those two hundred grams of minced steak.

Jenny I am.

Chris Not the dog then.

Jenny I'm sorry?

Chris Because 9 times out of 10 it's the dog. Guaranteed.

Slight pause.

Clair You should take off your hat.

Chris Mmm?

Clair Take off your hat. And don't wear your badge indoors. We know who you are.

Chris I'm Christopher. (*Grins.*)

Clair Exactly. You're my husband.

Chris I'm Christopher. I'm her husband. And I want my present. I don't want to take off my hat. I like my hat. I want my present.

Clair What makes you think I've got you a present?

Chris Well if she hasn't got me a present I'll break her fucking neck. (*Chuckles.*) Translate *that* into English—eh?

Clair I'll go and get it.

She goes. Pause.

Chris How's the war?

Jenny Mmm?

Chris The war. How's the war?

Jenny Oh, the war's fine, thank you.

Chris Going well?

Jenny Mmm?

Chris Going well, is it?

Jenny I think so.

Slight pause.

Chris And the enemy? How's the enemy?

Jenny Intractable.

Chris Oh?

Jenny Pretty intractable, yes.

Chris Bastards.

Slight pause.

Are you comfortable in those shoes?

Jenny What? Yes, I'm fine.

Chris Because if you're not comfortable / take them off.

Jenny I'm absolutely fine. Thank you.

Clair enters with gift.

Clair What is it?

Jenny Nothing.

Clair Is something wrong?

Jenny Of course not—no—we were chatting.

Chris What's this then?

Jenny Just chatting away.

Chris I said what's this?

Clair Open it.

He takes the present, opens it. It's the diary from Scene i.

Chris It's a diary.

Clair Yes.

Chris But it's been written in.

Clair Yes.

Chris Why's it been written in?

He flicks through the diary, stops at a page, reads softly.

'. . . a different person . . . to the person who is writing this now . . .' Hmm.

He flicks through, reads softly.

'. . . then I myself—this is what I imagined—could come . . .' (*Peers at word.*) What's this word?

Clair Alive—come alive.

Chris '. . . I myself—this is what I imagined—could come alive.' Hmm.

Pause. He looks at her.

Clair Go on.

Chris Go on what?

Jenny She means read it—don't you.

Clair Yes. Read it.

Chris reads softly, finding the words not always easy to decipher, following them with his finger. He's not a 'good' reader. He seems generally oblivious to the sense of what he's reading.

Chris 'When I was young—much younger than now— a different person you might even say—to the person who is writing this now—and before I began to make my living from translation—taking refuge in it as one writer says "the way an alcoholic takes refuge in alcoholism"— before that I truly believed there was . . .' (*Peers at word.*) Can't read it.

Clair A city.

Chris A what?

Clair A city.

Chris '. . . truly believed there was'—that's right—'a city inside of me—a huge and varied city full of green squares, shops and churches, secret streets, and hidden doors leading to staircases that climbed to rooms full of light where there would be drops of rain on the windows, and where in each small drop the whole city would be seen, upside down. There would be industrial zones where elevated trains ran past the windows of factories and conference centres. There would be schools where, when there was a lull in the traffic, you could hear children playing. The seasons in the city would be distinct: hot summer nights when everyone slept with their windows open, or sat out on their balconies in their underwear, drinking beer from the fridge—and in winter, very cold mornings when snow had settled in courtyards and they showed the snow on TV and the snow on TV was the same snow out in the street, shovelled to the side to enable the inhabitants to get to work. And I was convinced that in this city of mine I would find an inex . . .' (*Peers at word.*)

Clair Inexhaustible.

Chris '. . . an inexhaustible source of characters and stories for my writing. I was convinced that in order to be a writer I'd simply have to travel to this city—the one inside of me—and write down what I discovered there.'

Slight pause.

Clair Go on.

Chris 'I knew it would be difficult to reach this city. It wouldn't be like going on a plane to Marrakech, say, or Lisbon. I knew the journey could take days or even years quite possibly. But I knew that if I could find life in my city, and be able to describe life, the stories and characters of life, then I myself—this is what I imagined—could come alive. And I did reach my city. Yes. Oh yes. But when I reached it found it had been destroyed. The houses had been destroyed, and so had the shops. Minarets lay on the ground next to church steeples. What . . . balconies'? (*Momentarily confused.*) 'What balconies there were had dropped to the pavement. There were no children in the playgrounds, only coloured lines. I looked for inhabitants to write about, but there were no inhabitants, just dust. I looked for the people still clinging on to life—what stories they could tell!—but even there—in the drains, the basements—in the underground railway system—there was nothing—nobody—just dust. And this grey dust, like the ash from a cigarette, was so fine it got into my pen and stopped the ink reaching the page. Could this really be all that was inside of me? I cried at first but then I pulled myself together and tried for a while then to invent. I invented . . .' (*Peers at word.*) What?

Clair Characters.

Chris '. . . characters . . . invented characters . . .' (*Loses his place, finds it again.*) 'I invented characters and I put them in my city. The one I called Mohamed. The one I called the nurse—Jenny—she was funny. I invented a child too, I was quite pleased with the child. But it was a struggle. They wouldn't come alive. They lived a little—but only the way a sick bird tortured by a cat lives in a shoebox. It was hard to make them speak normally—and their stories fell apart even as I was telling them. Sometimes I even . . .' (*Peers at word.*) What's this?

Clair Dressed them up.

Chris Mmm?

Clair Dressed them—dressed / them up.

Chris 'Sometimes I even'—okay—'dressed them up the way I used to dress my dolls when I was little. I put them in funny clothes but then I felt ashamed. And when they looked at me, they looked at me—like it says in a book—"accusingly".'

The little girl appears, dressed exactly like Jenny: pink jeans, high-heeled shoes. She sits at the piano.

'So I gave up on my city. I was no writer—that much was clear. I'd like to say how sad the discovery of my own emptiness made me, but the truth is I feel as I write this down nothing but relief.'

He turns the pages looking for more text, but finds none. He closes the diary and looks at Clair.

What about me?

Clair What about you?

Chris Am I / invented too?

Clair Why don't you take off your hat now? What?

Chris Me. Am I invented too?

Clair No more than I am, surely. Take off your hat.

Jenny Yes. Go on. Take it off.

Chris Why?

Clair Because it will be better.

He slowly removes his hat.

You see: much better.

Chris You think?

Clair Much better. (*To Jenny.*) Don't you agree?

MARTIN CRIMP

Jenny Oh yes. Yes. Much better like that.

Clair (*to Girl*) Play us your piece, sweetheart.

Jenny Much much better like that.

> *The Girl begins to play the Schubert movement heard in Scene iii. She sets off confidently but gets stuck at bar 3. She starts again but is soon in difficulty. The light begins to fade. She can't get beyond bar 4.*

PLAY HOUSE

Play House was first performed in a double bill with
Definitely the Bahamas at the Orange Tree Theatre,
Richmond, on 14 March 2012. The cast was as follows:

Simon Obi Abili
Katrina Lily James

Director Martin Crimp
Designer Sam Dowson
Lighting Designer John Harris
Movement Joseph Alford
Assistant Director Karima Setohy
Assistant Designer Katy Mills

Characters

Simon
Katrina

Although there are thirteen distinct scenes, each with its own flavour, the performance should be continuous.

I DECLARATION (I)

— I love you so much. You fill the whole frame of my being. I go to sleep thinking about you and wake up with your voice winding through my head. Your eyes are so clear. If your eye was a well and I dropped a stone into it, that stone would never stop falling – I'm serious. I don't believe in God, but I do believe in you. I believe you created me. That's why I feel alive with you here – now – in our new home. Before I was just clay.

— You mean like a lump.

— Yes before I was just a lump of clay. But now I'm alive. You have created me. I'm serious.

She smiles.

You have an incredible smile.

She passes him a wrapped item.

What's this?

— Open it.

— For me?

— Open it.

He unwraps the gift: there's a cardboard box like a cake-box with a hinged lid. He raises the lid and reacts to the contents.

— What's this? Dog shit?

She tries not to laugh.

11 CLEANING THE FRIDGE

— I just had my mum on the phone.

— Your mum? What did your mum want?

— Oh – she's upset – seems my dad had a nervous breakdown. (*He looks at her.*) What?

— I didn't know people said that.

— Nervous breakdown? Of course they do.

They continue to clean the fridge.

— Is he in hospital?

— Of course they do. Because the trouble with you –

— Oh?

— Yes the trouble with you is you think you know better than everyone else.

They continue to clean the fridge.

You don't have to look so hurt. After all, this is not about you, Simon – it's about my dad – it's actually about my whole family. It's about a whole interconnected series of bad choices of which my dad's just one element. Because there's a whole cluster of genetic – well I won't go into that now – but also psychological and even political shit – a constellation of issues – adoption – attempted rape – within which my father is simply one faint star whose light barely reaches us.

Having *said* that –

— Oh?

— Yes having *said* that, I still don't trust her.

— Your mother?

— Well you've seen how she behaves. And since I moved in with you, she'll say anything to get my attention.

They continue to clean the fridge.

— About your dad?

— About herself. About her wasted life. About her fear for her own safety. Because – well – okay, Mister I-Know-Everything – you were right – it wasn't a 'nervous breakdown' – he had a psychotic episode.

Pause.

— Your dad did?

— Seems she woke up and found he'd set fire to the bedroom curtains. Oh shit.

— What?

— There's mould on this yoghurt.

— Chuck it.

III BRUSHING TEETH

— Where are you?

— (*Off.*) Brushing my teeth.

Pause.

— You know I was thinking about what you were saying.

— (*Off.*) What?

Pause.

— I said: I was thinking about what you were saying. About children? Katrina?

Pause.

Because on my way to the station I saw some going into the park. They were going in one at a time. In a row. Tiny ones. Are you listening?

Pause.

And what they had was a rope. Which they each held on to – so they wouldn't get lost. You should've heard them all chattering – holding on to this long blue rope. Because it's exactly what you were saying. About children. Katrina?

He gets up, now puzzled by her failure to react.

Katrina? I said: it's exactly the thing we were talking about.

He goes out. A moment passes.

(*Off, softly.*) Oh my God.

He returns with his arm round her shoulder. She has one hand up to her mouth, which is bloody.

Come on. Come on. Use this. What happened?

She dabs at her mouth with whatever he's given her.

What happened? Katrina?

She makes a gesture to be left alone, and goes on dabbing and spitting out blood.

IV HOME-ENTERTAINMENT

Very loud music: Wynonie Harris, 'My Playful Baby's Gone'.

Completely absorbed in one another, they dance.

Doorbell.

They take no notice. They go on dancing.

Doorbell again.

— (*Calls out.*) Go away! We're dancing!

Doorbell again.

I said go away!

They go on dancing. They get more and more into it.

Doorbell again.

— Fuck off!

— Fuck off!

— Go away! Fuck off!

Continuous doorbell.

They go on dancing, continuous doorbell just audible through the music. Finally Simon breaks away and goes off.

Doorbell stops but music continues.

He comes back, turns off the music, looks at her.

Silence.

— Who was it?

— No one.

— I love that song.

— Me too.

— What's that?

— (*Shrugs.*) Found it.

He's holding a card and a torn-open envelope. He brandishes the card and chuckles.

— What? What?

She tries to take the card, he snatches it back. They both play around with the card till she finally secures it. She reads it aloud.

'Dear neighbours, when I listen to you dancing or hear you make love, I so want to dance with you or make love too. You see you cannot imagine how –' What's that word?

— 'Unimaginably'.

— '– imagine how unimaginably'? – 'You cannot imagine how unimaginably hurt and – (*Turns card.*) – lonely I am. But I am not asking for your pity. No. Do not pity me. I just need you to know that I exist and think your lives must be beautiful. Ian.'

— Ian? Who's Ian?

— Or it could be Jon – or Jan perhaps. It could say Jan.

— A woman?

V MOBILE DEVICE (1)

Simon consults a mobile device throughout.

— Well of course sometimes it was bad. Sometimes
when he was drunk it would just go on and on
and I'd be thinking I'm not enjoying this, please let
it stop. But at other times I was excited and did it
because I loved him. He was my first love and I loved
him. I was calm and relaxed with him – then tense.
I needed his approval but at the same time wanted to
drive a bolt through his forehead like they do in a
slaughterhouse. He said: well go on then – try it.
Then got down on all fours like an animal. (*She
smiles.*) God my dad hated him.

What is it you're doing?

— Mmm?

— I said what is it you're / doing?

— (*Not looking up from device.*) Well you know how
Kant said you should never lie – even if a soldier
comes into your house and asks where your children
are – I mean with the intention of killing them – and
Kant said you must never lie – you must say, Well my
children are in the wardrobe – or – I don't know – my
children are out in the garden, playing on the swing.
Well I'm just checking that Kant actually said that.

He carries on tapping the tiny keys.

VI   MOBILE DEVICE (2)

No apparent change from Scene v. Simon is tapping at the same mobile device. Silence apart from the tapping.

— Huh!

— What?

— The battery's dead.

— It can't be.

— What're you doing?

— I want to see.

— You don't need to see. I'm telling you: it's dead.

— Don't talk to me like that.

— I'm sorry?

— Don't talk to me in that condescending way. Who d'you think you are?

— The battery's dead. I don't need confirmation.

— But it's brand new. It's a brand new phone, Simon. I spent money on that! Come on. Show me.

He gives her the phone. She deftly takes it apart, removing the battery etc.

— What's wrong with us? Why can't we say or do or think one single thing of importance? How is it that day after day after day can go by and not one word we speak makes any difference to the sum total of human thought? Mmm?

— (*Concentrating on phone.*) Rubbish. Who says there has to be a sum total?

— But what is the point of making us so complicated as beings when even my cat poking its head over the side of its cat box has more dignity than I do?

— (*As before.*) You don't have a cat, Simon.

— I did when I was a boy.

— But you're not a boy now, are you – (*She tosses him the phone.*) It works. – You're a man. You're a man and everything you say is important, and everything you think has consequences. Look at us. Like it or not we're in charge of the whole universe – from the precessionary stars to each dim sheep tottering through the valley.

— Including cats.

— Including – you're so totally right – cats. So don't let's pretend we have no responsibility. Because like it or not, we're the ones running the whole show.

Pause.

— You mean you are.

She laughs.

VII HOME FROM WORK

— (*Excited.*) You'll never guess what happened.

— (*Excited.*) What?

— I bumped into Jan on the stairs.

— Who?

Pause.

(*Realises.*) Oh my God. Jan. What happened? Did you say something?

— I said 'I hope our music isn't disturbing you.'

Both crease up with laughter.

— But how did you know it was her?

— Mmm?

— How did you know it was her? – Jan?

— Mmm?

— How did you know who it was?

— She was wearing ID. She works in a shop. I mean works in a bank. She works in a bank. I've no idea why I said / shop.

— Which bank?

— The . . . the . . . Hong Kong and Shanghai.

— Okay. So what did she say?

— Mmm?

— About the music. Come on. Wake up!

— About the music?

— Yes. About the music.

— Said she never hears it.

— (*Faint laugh.*) Lying little bitch.

— Where're you going?

— Lying little eavesdropping fucking bank-clerk bitch –

— Katrina –

— What? What?

Slight pause.

— She's not a clerk. She sells Credit Default Swaps to Scandinavian hedge-funds

Slight pause.

— Then what is she doing living in a shit-hole like this?

Slight pause.

— If you mean, why does she have only a modest apartment like ours – that's because she's basically based in Stockholm. This is just a pied-à-terre.

Slight pause.

Katrina, please don't cry.

Long pause. She wipes her eyes.

— I'm not.

— Difficult day?

— Mmm. [= *yes*]

— Those students again?

— Mmm. [= *yes*]

— You should separate the ringleaders.

— I'm going to.

Pause.

What? (*Amused.*) Why are you staring at me like that? Stop it. Stand normally. Uncross your arms. What?

— Well listen, you may or may not approve of this, but the thing is she gave me some pills. And you know what it's like when someone has a particularly strong personality and you want to obey them so you do what they say almost in spite of yourself? Because I said to her: look, Jan, I don't take drugs from strange women. And Jan said: that's only because you don't work in international finance and may never have had the opportunity. D'you see? She was quite funny – as well as very persuasive. She said to me: I normally take three, but two is enough to start with.

Pause.

— And you took them?

— What?

— These pills – these pills from this ghastly bank woman – you / took them?

— Of course not. (*Unfolds his arms.*) They're still here – in my fist.

— Show me.

— But the thing is – yes the odd thing is – is since talking to Jan – who's not at all ghastly by the way – but since talking to Jan – even without the pills – I already feel that my mind has completely altered.

— (*Slaps his face.*) Show me. (*Slaps his face again.*)

— Hey!

— Open your hand, Simon!

She slaps his face again – struggles to open his fist – then gives up.

— And of course you're quite right: there is part of me that's not sure whether I've taken those pills or not. There is part of me that's wondering just what is inside this fist.

VIII POST-COITAL

Simon watches Katrina trying to do handstands.

— What're you doing?

She keeps trying.

Katrina?

— I used to be able to do this.

She keeps trying.

— You're going to break something.

— You take my legs.

— I don't want to take your legs.

— Yes you do. Go on. Please.

She stands on her hands – he takes her legs.

— I've got your thighs in my face.

— You should like it.
I can feel it.
I'm definitely getting pregnant.

— It's nothing to do with which way up you are.

— You're so funny. I love you.

She laughs.

— What?

— The sockets have little faces. And the chair looks
glued to the ceiling.
Well come on.

— Come on what?

— Say you love me too.

— I love you too.

— Even though you're upside down.

— Even though you're upside down.

— Even though THE WHOLE WORLD is upside down.
Say it.

— (*Amused.*) Stop kicking my head.

— Then say it!

— What're you doing?

— I'm climbing you.

— Jesus. Katrina – this is dangerous.

— Then say that the whole world's upside down.

— But it's not. The whole world is not upside down –
you're the one who is / upside down.

— Oh stop being such a literal-minded . . . un-poetic . . .
fucking . . . / planning-officer!

— Then just stop . . . climbing all over me . . . Katrina!
For God sake!

They collapse on the floor laughing and kissing.

IX VISITOR (1)

Pause.

— But what was he doing here? I don't understand that
he just turned up – I thought he was still sick. How
long did he stay for? Simon?

— Maybe an hour?

— An hour? He has no right. He has no right turning up
here imposing his problems. (*Slight pause.*) What did
he talk about?

— I promised not to say.

— Was it about me? What d'you mean: you promised?

— I promised I wouldn't say.

— Was he talking about me? Mmm?

— Not everything is about you.

— I do realise that. I naturally realise that. But why did he bring the dress? (*Slight pause.*) I mean that's just so completely weird having my dad turn up here with that dress. Dad never turns up anywhere. Dad never talks to anyone. And for a whole *hour*?

— I wish I hadn't told you now.

— (*Picks up dress.*) I haven't worn this since I was fourteen.

She toys with the dress: Simon watches her. The emotions associated with the dress pass through her body.

— (*Smiles.*) Look: let's do a deal. I say what he said – and you do the thing we talked about.

— What thing we talked about? (*Realises and laughs.*) You must be joking. I'm not 'doing a deal' with you. Especially about that. I've told you: it's no. Never. Not ever. It just doesn't interest me.

— (*Shrugs.*) Okay.

— Well it doesn't.

— Okay. You've told me.

— I'm putting this on a hanger.

— Sure.

She goes out.

X PROMOTION

Simon alone, cheerful. Wearing headphones, he hums or whistles to himself snatches of the tune from Scene iv, half dancing.

Katrina comes in with some bags and watches. Finally he spots her and takes the headphones off.

Big smiles.

— Hey.

— Hey.

— Well.

— Yes.

— Great. Wow.

— Yes.

— You must be . . . [*thrilled*]

— I am.

— Wow. Weird.

— No. [= *not really*] Yes? [= *d'you think?*]

— Kind of. I mean Head of . . .

— Department – yes.

— Great. They . . . [*told you today*]?

— That's right.

— Amazing.

— [*I*] Got the call and . . .

— Shit. [= *amazing*]

216

— Got the call and . . . Yes – shit.

— Wow.

Pause. Faint sound of music from the headphones. Katrina becomes aware of this and turns the music player off.

— Hey come here.

— What?

— Just come here.

— (*Teasing.*) *Oh* no.

— Come on.

— *Oh* no.

— Hey . . .

— I know what you want.

— Oh? What's that?

— (*Teasing.*) *So* predictable.
Turn around.

— What?

— Turn around. Go on.

He turns his back.

— What's going on?

She gets a wrapped present out of one of her bags and puts it down. It resembles the wrapped present from Scene i.

— Okay, you can look.

— What's that?

— Open it.

— For me?

— Yes. Open it.

He takes it and starts to unwrap it. Sudden thought:

— It's not?

— Not what?

— Nothing.

— Hmm?

— Nothing.

He finishes unwrapping: it's a tie.

(*With admiration.*) Hey!

— Like it?

— That is stylish. Thank you.

He kisses her gently on the lips.

— So is this going to mean more . . . ?

— Sex?

— (*Playful.*) What? No. Stupid. Money.

— Sure.

— Money.

— Sure. Yes.

— Great.

He moves away from her to examine the tie.

— But it's more it's the . . .

— Of course.

— . . . more it's the . . . accolade. Because turns out I am the youngest –

— Wow.

— Yes I'm the youngest – ever – Deputy Head of Commercial Planning.

He looks up from the tie. They both smile at each other.

— I am so incredibly happy.

— Thank you.

XI SELF-ASSEMBLY

Katrina is using an electric screwdriver to finish assembling a small self-assembly table.

Simon is reading through some documents, from time to time glancing at her.

— What is that for?

— I said – to put the lamp on.

— Great.

She completes the table, and stands it on its legs.

Nice.

Pause.

Is something wrong, Katrina? Has something happened?

— Such as?

— Well . . . maybe that man-friend of yours turned up at the school and you finally decided to butcher him.

She puts the lamp on the table and adjusts its position. Then:

— You think I've got blood on my hands?

— Show me.

She holds up her hands – like 'surrender'.

— You were probably wearing gloves.
I'd've loved seeing him drop to his knees.
Fucked over by the goddess of destruction.

— Destruction? I've just built us a table, Simon.

She plugs in the lamp and switches it on.

XII VISITOR (2)

Simon is wearing the tie from Scene x.

— I'm a bit drunk.

— Me too.

She looks at her watch.

Okay. Ten thirty. Now you have to tell me what my dad said.

— Oh no I do not.

— Oh yes you do.

— But she's not going to come.

— That wasn't the deal. The deal was: I asked. You've still got that tie on. I thought I said take it off.

He fiddles with the tie, but leaves it on.

There's food down it.

— Yes but how do I know you asked?

— I just did. I told you I did. If I told you I did, I did.

— And what did she say again?

— She said yes she would love to, and what should she bring? So I said bring some of those pills you gave to my husband.

— Maybe she didn't understand.

— Oh she understood. She got it just like that. I could see her assessing me. Then she smiled and reached out for my mouth.

— You didn't say she reached out for your mouth.

— Well she did – she slipped in her finger and hooked it right over my teeth.

Pause.

— Why 're you smiling like that?

— Because you don't love me. Because you have never loved me. I've given you my whole body and all of my attention for months and months and months – and it's still not enough for you. I've given you my hopefulness and all of my wit and charm, my tolerance and a large part of my pitiful income – and it's still not enough. I've listened to you tell me how meaningless your life is – regardless of how much that insults me personally – and I've heard you out for hours on end about the struggle for desk-space within your department. I've shut up while you've insulted a man I very much loved – and to please you, I've forced myself to leave no space for him in my heart. And all

of that time – while I was giving you everything –
you've been chipping and chipping away at my soul
until I have finally said yes to something so humiliating
and so banal that I feel – yes I do, Simon – you don't
have to look so hurt – feel like swallowing acid.

Pause.

— I see. No wonder you're smiling.

Pause.

So you want me to take off my tie.

— No what I want is to spit in your face.

— Well you won't manage that from there.

— Then come closer. Come on. Closer.

*He crawls towards her on all fours. She spits in his
face.*

— Bitch.

— Pig.

The doorbell rings.

Katrina gets up with sudden efficiency and excitement.

Oh my God! Wipe your face. Get up off the floor,
idiot. I'll let her in. You pour her a drink.

XIII DECLARATION (2)

Katrina is bending over a cardboard box making faint friendly nonsense sounds. She is wearing the dress from Scene ix.

— Doo doo doo doo doo – boo boo boo – coo coo – doo doo doo – (*Etc.*)

Simon appears and watches her.

— What's that?

— It's my dress. D'you like it?

Katrina resumes nonsense sounds.

— I meant what's that in the basket?

— What does it look like?

— A baby? Where did you get a baby from?

Katrina resumes nonsense sounds.

I said where did you get a baby from?

— Where d'you think I got a baby from?

Katrina resumes nonsense sounds.

— I thought we didn't want children.

— Oh? (*Smiles.*) No – I think we decided we did.

Katrina resumes nonsense sounds.

— Is it a boy or a girl?

— Does it matter?

— Wouldn't you prefer a girl?

— Why would I prefer a girl?
Wouldn't I just be endlessly dreading the day some
man came and took her away from me – married her –
and forced her to play house? How could I bear
visiting her up a flight of stone stairs nobody ever
washed – where all the lights in the hallway, Simon,
were smashed – or – if on – dim? How would I cope
with holding her baby for just a few minutes – then
having to leave before her husband came back, so
she'd not have to see how much I despised him?

Katrina resumes nonsense sounds. Long long pause.

— Yes – but what if she turned out – Katrina – against
all the odds – to be happy? What if she secretly liked
to play house? What if the . . . broken bicycle on the
stairs – or even the burst black sack – made her smile?
And this man – what if this man of hers – the
husband – with his shit job and all the other shit
infecting his mind – what if he still truly loved her?
Yes loved her and loved her – and loved her and
loved her and loved her. What if he loved her at the
end as much as he had loved her at the beginning?
What if he had dropped once into her eyes – and was
still falling?

DEFINITELY THE BAHAMAS

Definitely the Bahamas was first performed in a production for BBC Radio 3 broadcast in April 1987. The cast was as follows:

Milly Rosemary Leach
Frank Norman Bird
Marijke Holly de Jong

Directed by John Tydeman

The play was subsequently staged at the Orange Tree Theatre, Richmond, opening on 25 September 1987. The cast was as follows:

Milly Heather Canning
Frank John Moffat
Marijke Amanda Royle
A Friend Rob Edwards

Directed by Alec McCowen

The play was revived in a double bill with *Play House* at the Orange Tree Theatre, Richmond, on 14 March 2012. The cast was as follows:

Milly Kate Fahy
Frank Ian Gelder
Marijke Lily James
A Technician Obi Abili

Director Martin Crimp
Designer Sam Dowson
Lighting Designer John Harris
Assistant Director Karima Setohy
Assistant Designer Katy Mills

Characters

Milly
late fifties

Frank
early sixties

Marijke
late teens

Marijke is Dutch, but speaks English
with a scarcely perceptible accent. Dutch words,
however, including her own name, she pronounces
with characteristic Dutch intonation.

Frank and Milly both pronounce her name 'Marika',
with the same rhythm and short 'i' as 'juniper'.

Passages enclosed between half-brackets ⌈thus⌋ indicate where Milly and Frank address lines exclusively to each other and to nobody else.

Phrases such as 'Don't you Frank', 'Isn't it Frank', are included in these brackets only when a response is clearly expected.

Long silence.

Milly It's so quiet here. It was the first thing we noticed, wasn't it Frank.

Frank ⌈What's that?

Milly The quiet. I say it's the first thing we noticed.⌋ Because we were going out of our minds in the other place. I said to Frank, didn't I Frank, I said we're going out of our minds here.

Frank Mill couldn't stand the aeroplanes.

Milly ⌈Nor could you.⌋ Nor could Frank. Oh he says he didn't notice but of course he did. Because I said to him it can't be good for your nerves, didn't I Frank, and then we saw a programme and they said it's a psychological fact that that kind of noise is bad for your nerves. ⌈Didn't they Frank.⌋

Frank Of course that was with rats.

Milly ⌈Well yes, I know it was with rats Frank, but still it's a psychological fact, that's my point.⌋ (*Pause.*) But when we arrived here the first thing we did was go into the garden, didn't we Frank, because it was summer and the flowers were glorious then. And Frank took my arm, which is unusual for him, and he said to me listen, didn't you Frank, listen. And I said what do you mean Frank, listen. And he said, nothing, just listen.

Long silence.

231

Milly Irene* and Michael liked it straight away, didn't they.

Frank Mike was very impressed.

Milly And they're very critical, aren't they Frank. They have very high standards. Because of course Michael's done so terribly well for himself. They've got an enormous place, haven't they Frank.

Frank Several acres.

Milly And Irene's done some wonderful things to the house. She's very daring, isn't she Frank, when it comes to colours. Not that I could live with some of her ideas. I've said to her, it's very imaginative Irene, but I couldn't live with it.

   Pause.

Getting in's such a performance, isn't it Frank. Because before they'll open the gates to the drive you have to talk through a loudspeaker, and I hate talking into those things, don't I Frank.

Frank A microphone, she means.

Milly ⌈A what?⌋

Frank You have to ring the bell and speak through a microphone.

Milly ⌈That's not what Irene calls it.

Frank Well that's what it is.

Milly Well that's not what she calls it.⌋ (*Slight pause.*) They got it after the break-in. That and the alarm. It means Irene feels a lot safer when she's on her own. ⌈ She's always called it the loudspeaker. Surely she should know.⌋ The break-in was a terrible blow.

---

* They pronounce 'Irene' as two syllables.

Frank They were certainly thorough.

Milly It shook them. It really did. It shook Irene.

Frank And the thing was they were away in the Bahamas at the time.

Milly The Canaries he means.

Frank ⌈I thought it was the Bahamas.

Milly Well yes they were going to go to the Bahamas, but then if you remember at the last moment something cropped up and they went to the Canaries instead.⌋ But as I say it really shook them.

Frank ⌈It was definitely the Bahamas.⌋

Milly And the tragedy was they weren't fully insured, not when it came to the small print. I thought that was very unlike Michael, not to have looked at the small print.

Slight pause.

Frank ⌈It was definitely the Bahamas, Mill. And I'll tell you why: we had a phone call from Miami.

Milly I don't remember any phone call from Miami.⌋

Frank It was to tell us they'd arrived.

Milly ⌈Why would they bother to tell us they've arrived in Miami, when they're going to the Bahamas?

Frank Because they were stopping off to see their friends.

Milly Well if by that you mean Poppy and Max, then they wouldn't've been stopping off in Miami because it's years since Poppy and Max lived in Miami. If you remember Frank, they'd moved to Tenerife. They'd already bought their villa in Tenerife.⌋

Pause.

Frank It was mainly their appliances. They were very thorough as I say.

Milly And the shock of course.

Frank Because naturally they had all the time in the world.

Milly And then what with Irene losing her baby after.

Frank They'd even been for a spin in the BMW. Mike was very upset about that.

Milly Losing her baby and only back home three days.

Frank He says it still makes his blood boil to think of them joyriding in his BMW.

Pause.

⌈I don't know why you're looking at me like that because of course it was tragic⌋ but I've said to Mill we can't be certain the break-in was the cause. (*Slight pause.*) My own theory is the plane.

Milly Of course I went straight down to be with her. Michael had to go off with the firm.

Frank Something to do with the pressure.

Milly It broke his heart naturally, but his position was at stake, wasn't it Frank.

Frank Something to do with the pressurisation of the cabin, that's my theory.

Milly Because when you're in that sort of business there are always people only too willing to step into your shoes at a moment's notice. Irene says the pressure can be quite frightening, doesn't she Frank.

Frank Because I've been into it in some detail, and although the cabin is pressurised as of course it would have to be at that altitude, the fact of the matter is there's a significant differential between the atmospheric pressure at sea level and the pressure in a jumbo say flying at forty thousand feet.

Milly Frank's been into it all. In the library.

Pause.

She'd got such a lovely tan as well. Irene's so lucky the way she tans like that. Of course she's got the sunbed too. Having a sunbed must help. Provided you don't overdo the ultra-violet. (*Slight pause.*) ⌈Where are those pictures, Frank?⌋ We've got some nice ones of them somewhere. ⌈Weren't you going to get them out, Frank?⌋ He told me he was going to get them out. (*Slight pause.*) I won't be a moment then.

Silence as Milly goes.

Frank (*more relaxed in Milly's absence*) It was quite definitely the Bahamas as a matter of fact. Oh yes it's perfectly true that Max and Poppy moved to Tenerife – Mike and Max met up while they were out in Cape Town by the way – because of course they went there, Tenerife I mean, when their dog was killed.

Milly (*from another room*)⌈I can't see them, Frank.⌋

Frank Because they'd always felt like having a stab at Tenerife, but while they still had the dog –

Milly (*as before*) ⌈I said I can't see them, Frank.

Frank (*raising voice*) Didn't you have them out when Joan was here?⌋ (*Slight pause. Relaxed again.*) Where was I? Oh yes I was saying, while they still had their Doberman there was no question of moving on account of the additional cost, not to mention the sheer size of it.

And Max had a passion for that animal evidently. Mike said he wouldn't've left her behind for anything. But anyway it was rather gruesome as it turned out, because when they eventually found her, the Doberman I mean, the head had been hacked off. And the interesting thing was was it wasn't an isolated incident, because –

Milly (*as before*) ⌈You're not talking about that dog are you, Frank?⌉

Slight pause.

Frank It wasn't an isolated incident because drugs were involved and when the police finally cracked down on them –

Milly (*as before*) ⌈You know I don't like you talking about that dog.⌋

Slight pause.

Frank When they finally cracked down on them the interesting thing was was they were only children. Eight years old I think the youngest was. Max told Mike they were getting 'high' on these drugs and drinking the blood or something of the kind, I'm not sure of the exact details. Anyway it meant the two of them, Max and Poppy I mean, were very keen to move away, particularly with this 'cult' or whatever it was right on their doorstep so to speak. And since they'd always fancied a stab at Tenerife as I say, they were out by the end of the month. And I believe they're very happy there. They've got several acres, and a pool. At least I think there's a pool. Mill will know if there's a pool or not.

Milly (*entering room*) ⌈What will Mill know?

Frank If there's a pool.⌋

Milly Oh yes there's quite a big pool.

Pause.

He knows I don't like him talking about that dog.

Pause.

I'd love a pool you know. Frank says what's the use of a pool when I can't swim but I've told him if I had a pool I'd learn. And I don't know why he's looking at me like that ⌈because I would Frank if I say I would. Marijke could've taught me for one thing.⌋ (*Slight pause.*) And besides you don't have to go in. There's no one making you go in. I've said to Frank surely one of the pleasures of having your own pool is sitting on the side, just looking at the water. I could spend all day looking at water.

Pause.

And of course Marijke could've used it. She could've brought her friends. Because sometimes I worry about her going on her own to the public baths. Because let's face it you never know what sort of people you're going to find in a place like that, do you Frank.

Pause.

Frank says he's getting too old to dig a pool, but I've told him why don't we get a man in, I really can't imagine what he has against having a man in. Because Irene doesn't think twice about having a man in. And it needn't be heated. Irene's isn't heated but she manages.

Long silence.

(*With enthusiasm.*) That's Irene barbecuing the chops. ⌈ It's a good one of her, isn't it Frank.⌋ It's very typical of Irene, that smile. It's so natural. That's me in the background behind the smoke.

Slight pause.

237

(*Faint laugh.*) That's Michael being stupid showing off his tan. ⌈Where had they been, Frank?

Frank Wasn't it South Africa?⌋

Milly Yes that's right, they'd been back to see friends in Cape Town. Because of course they made a lot of friends over there in their South African days.

Frank And a lot of money.

Milly Oh yes they made a lot of money because they worked hard and they went at the right time. But it hasn't changed them, has it Frank. Because of course Michael has a head for business. If he didn't have a head for business he wouldn't be where he is today. But do you know he's still a romantic at heart, isn't he Frank. Whenever he rang home he was always enthusing about the beautiful scenery they have over there. The mountains. The wildlife. We've got some pictures somewhere.

Slight pause.

This is me next to the pool. Irene's flip-flops gave me blisters. That's why I'm pulling such a face. ⌈Really Frank, you could've waited till I'd made myself decent.⌋

Slight pause.

Now this is meant to be Michael diving in, but Frank missed him, didn't you Frank. Still, it's a nice one of the pool. The black and orange tiles were Irene's idea. They're rather effective actually.

Slight pause.

Oh now this gives you some idea of the grounds. Everything you can see is theirs, up to the barbed wire fence.

Slight pause.

238

That's Frank trying Michael's snorkel on. It's funny,
Frank never comes out well in pictures. ⌈Do you Frank.

Slight pause.

What's this one, Frank?

Frank (*slight pause as he looks*) Isn't it Michael with
Marijke?

Milly I didn't know we had one of Michael and Marijke.

Frank It must be when Michael and Irene were here for
Easter.

Milly I didn't know we had a picture. (*Faint laugh.*) Just
look at them. I didn't think it was warm enough for
sprawling on the lawn like that.⌋

Slight pause.

(*With enthusiasm.*) No I didn't realise we had a picture
of Michael and Marijke. Irene must've taken it. It's a
nice surprise, because of course the two of them hit it off
rather well when they were up for Easter. Michael's been
to Germany, you see. He's been all over on business.

Frank Marijke's Dutch.

Milly ⌈I know Marijke's Dutch. Of course Marijke's
Dutch. But she's been to Germany and she understands
German, that's my point.⌋ They all do, the Germans
I mean the Dutch, they all have a wonderful gift for
languages. Marijke's Dutch for example is quite
remarkable.

Frank ⌈You mean her English.

Milly I said her English.

Frank You said her Dutch.

Milly Well I meant her English. Obviously she speaks
Dutch. She is Dutch.

Frank I'm just saying what you said.

Milly Well does it matter, Frank? Does it really matter what I said?⌋ Of course, I meant her English. ⌈Obviously I meant her English.

Frank And it wasn't German.

Milly I know. It was English. I made a mistake that's all.⌋

Frank It wasn't German, it was Afrikaans.

Milly ⌈Afrikaans?

Frank Yes.⌋

Pause.

Milly Well anyway what was I saying, oh yes she and Michael hit it off like a house on fire what with both of them being able to speak German or whatever it was – ⌈ I really don't see that it matters, Frank⌋ – which was very nice for Marijke, because she often seems a little sulky, and sometimes I don't think she finds it easy to make friends over here, probably on account of the language problem as I say, which is a shame because she's such a pretty girl really, or at least she could be if she didn't wear those dreadful skirts with a slit all the way up the side, couldn't she Frank.

Both with mounting amusement.

Frank But the funniest thing was the flowers he bought her . . .

Milly Oh those flowers were a scream. I nearly died, didn't I Frank.

Frank Because he bought her a huge bunch of tulips . . .

Milly Tulips, can you imagine . . .

Frank Mike can be a real comedian when he wants to be . . .

Milly It was so nice to see Marijke letting herself go for a change . . .

Frank I really didn't think that sofa was going to be able to take it . . .

Milly And they were both in such a state with the giggles I don't think they even realised we were watching. There were flowers all over the place . . .

Frank (*with relish*) It looked for a moment as if the whole thing was going to collapse . . . (*Laughs.*)

Milly (*with relish*) It's a wonder to me they didn't both end up on the floor . . . (*Laughs.*)

Frank and Milly laugh at length. Laughter ends.

Oh dear . . . (*Faint after-laugh.*)

Pause.

It's a shame Frank doesn't have a flash.

Frank Of course Irene wouldn't have them in the house.

Milly She's got some terrible allergies, Irene. With me it's cats.

Pause.

⌈Where is Marijke anyway?

Frank Isn't she vacuuming?

Milly I can't hear the vacuum.

Pause.

No I can't hear the vacuum. Are you sure she's vacuuming?⌋

(*Calls.*) Marijke. Marijke.

Pause.

Michael invited her down which was rather charming of him. And he always mentions it when he rings. When's Marijke coming down, he says. We'd love to see her again before she goes back to Holland. (*Calls.*) Marijke.

Pause.

⌐Are you sure she's in?

Frank I thought she was vacuuming.

Milly Yes but have you seen her?⌐

Frank She often vacuums on Saturdays.

Milly ⌐Yes but I don't think she is vacuuming, Frank. That's my point.⌐

Pause.

Of course it was after their first trip to the Cape that Michael started carrying a gun. Because Irene was nearly raped over there. I wish he wouldn't but he says he owes it to Irene.

Pause.

Frank It wasn't actually a rape.

Milly ⌐Well it was nearly a rape.⌐

Frank What happened was this black chap knocked her down in a street and snatched her handbag.

Milly Well if that's not nearly a rape I'd like to know what is. Because it's certainly violence of the lowest kind.

Frank It was registered as a robbery.

Milly ⌐Yes but that's the police. What do the police know?⌐ They're too soft if you ask me. And the unfortunate thing was she'd only just been to the bank.

Frank They think he followed her.

Milly Well of course he followed her. It was quite premeditated. And this was broad daylight, can you imagine? Nearly raped in broad daylight. Where were the police, that's what I'd like to know. Why didn't they catch him, that's what I'd like to know. I really think they're too soft on these sexual offenders.

Frank There doesn't seem to've been a sexual motive.

Milly Well I really don't know how Frank can sit there and say there wasn't a sexual motive. Because why did he knock her down if there wasn't a sexual motive? Why didn't he just snatch the bag and run? No it's quite clear to me he knocked her down because of the sexual motive and then perhaps he thought he heard someone coming because it was broad daylight after all and decided to run off with the bag instead. Because Michael's been in this very room and he's told us, even if Frank now chooses to forget, but he's told us how it's a psychological fact that the only thing a black man wants to do over there is sleep with a white woman, which is why of course there used to be laws against it before all these reforms.

Frank ⌈I think you'll find that view of Mike's is rather extreme, Mill.

Milly Well maybe it is Frank. Maybe it is extreme. But I really don't see what position you're in to argue with a psychological fact, because you're not a black man or a white woman are you,⌋ and it's all very well to say it's extreme but I can remember Irene telling us, in this very room, although perhaps Frank wasn't paying any attention, but I can remember her saying how she felt when she saw the look in his eyes. Like meat on a slab, that's what she said.

Frank It's actually what Mike said.

Milly (*decisively*) Like meat on a butcher's slab Frank, I don't care who said it.

Long silence.

Marijke (*from the doorway throughout*) Did you want me, Mrs Taylor?

Milly Ah there you are Marijke. We were just having a debate about where you were.

Pause.

Where did you find that towel?

Marijke It was in the airing cupboard.

Milly But isn't it one of Frank's? Really I wish she wouldn't just pick up the first one that comes to hand. It's a terrible habit she has.

Marijke I didn't realise.

Milly Because maybe I could understand her taking one of mine, but surely she can see the writing on it. 'His' is Frank's, Marijke.

Pause.

We thought you were vacuuming.

Marijke I've been to the baths, Mrs Taylor. Then I washed my hair.

Milly [She wasn't vacuuming Frank, she was washing her hair.] (*Slight pause.*) Was it nice at the baths?

Marijke Yes it was nice at the baths, but there was a great deal of activity.

Milly Well there would be, wouldn't there Frank, there would be a great deal of . . . activity, on a Saturday morning.

Pause.

We were just saying how well you and Michael hit it off at Easter. We found a photograph.

Marijke Hit it off?

Milly Yes, you remember Michael.

Marijke May I see?

Pause.

Milly I was saying to Frank I didn't know the weather had been good enough for lounging on the lawn like that, but I suppose it must've been.

Marijke (*in the room: faint laugh of recollection*)

Milly Try not to drip over it, Marijke. (*Slight pause.*) It's a shame it's not clearer, but I don't think Irene understands Frank's camera. Mind you nor does Frank all the time, do you Frank. (*Slight pause.*) And talking of dripping. Marijke. Marijke please don't walk off while I'm speaking. It's a terrible habit she has walking off while you're speaking. (*Slight pause.*) I say talking of dripping, please mind where you put your wet things. She has a habit of leaving her wet things all over the place. (*Slight pause.*) Off you go then.

Silence as Marijke goes.

You see she really could be quite presentable if she didn't insist on dressing like that. Because there's nothing uglier to my mind than seeing all of a girl's thighs, don't you think. [Don't you think, Frank.] (*Slight pause.*) You know I don't think he even notices. [Do you.

Frank What's that?

Milly Marijke's legs. You don't even notice, do you.] You see, he doesn't even notice.

Frank [(*absently*) What's wrong with her legs?]

Milly You see.

Pause.

(*Faint laugh*.) Activity. Really, Marijke does have an odd way of speaking sometimes, doesn't she Frank. (*Slight pause. With concern*.) ⌈Are you alright Frank? You look a little peaky.⌋ Doesn't he – look a little peaky. ⌈Is it your nerves again?⌋ Frank suffers with his nerves. ⌈Don't you Frank.⌋ So does Irene funnily enough. They've both been through hell and high water with their nerves. And do you know it turns out they both have the same pills. It was such a coincidence wasn't it Frank. But really of course it's a blessing for all concerned, because it means if we go to visit or they come here and one of them's forgotten their pills, then it's not the disaster it might've been. ⌈Is it Frank. (*Slight pause*.) Do you want to go and lie down for a while? (*Slight pause*.) No? Are you sure? Have you had your pill?⌋ (*Slight pause*.) Of course I think this year the weather's had a lot to do with it. Because the winter was bitter here, really bitter, and then when spring came well it never really warmed up did it Frank, it was one dismal day after another except perhaps for one or two fine April mornings when the rain held off, but even then you couldn't go out without tights on, could you Frank. And so not surprisingly we'd set our hearts on having something of a summer but now look here we are it's nearly the end of August, and do you know I don't think we've had so much as one really fine day, have we Frank, not one really glorious summer's day in all these months. ⌈And I know what you're going to say Frank: what good would it've done me to have a pool.⌋ But the fact is a pool would've been some compensation.

Pause. Having started during the previous speech, a telephone is very faintly audible, ringing in another room.

⌈Is that the telephone, Frank? (*Slight pause*.) Frank.

Frank Yes?

Milly It's the phone.

Frank Do you want me to go?

Milly Won't Marijke go?

Frank I'm quite happy to go.⌋

Pause as Frank goes. Faint ringing persists.

Milly Really he didn't have to go. She's quite capable of answering the phone. More often than not it's for Marijke these days. Not that I'm complaining. Because she could be worse. Frank and I thought it would be far worse to have a teenager always under our feet. Loud music. Boyfriends. Long baths. Needless scenes. But in fact she's turned out far better than we'd expected, even if she is a little sulky sometimes. And of course it's been very useful to have someone to help with the house when she's not at college. I've said to Frank, we'll be quite lost when she goes. (*Slight pause.*) Because the fact is we would've liked a bigger family. We never intended to stop at just the one. Not that we didn't try. Well I tried. Well what I mean is of course we both tried, only . . . (*Slight pause. Raising voice.*) ⌈Who was it Frank?

Frank (*entering room*) A callbox.

Milly A callbox?

Frank He couldn't get through.

Milly Who do we know in a callbox, Frank?⌋

Frank He couldn't get through.

Telephone ringing again as before. A moment passes. Marijke answers.

Marijke (*very faintly, from another room*) Hello? (*Pause. Faint laughter. Pause. Faint laughter.*)

Marijke continues to speak on the phone, just audible at pauses. However nothing she says is intelligible at this distance.

Frank (*in response to Marijke's laughter.*) Sounds like one of her men-friends.

Milly ⌐I beg your pardon, Frank? (*Slight pause.*)

Frank Alec or one of those.

Milly Alec's just a boy, Frank. He's a boy, not a man.

Frank Well of course he's a boy.

Milly Then why did you use that expression?⌐ (*Slight pause.*) He knows I hate that expression. It always puts me in mind of a particular sort of woman.

Frank ⌐It sounded like Alec.⌐ I say, I'm sure it was only Alec or one of those.

Milly ⌐What do you mean it sounded like Alec?

Frank The first time he rang. I thought I recognised the voice the first time he rang.

Milly But I thought he couldn't get through?

Frank Well when I said he couldn't get through what I meant was was there was something wrong with the line.⌐ Because I could hear him, but he didn't seem able to hear me.

Milly ⌐Well why didn't you say?

Frank It seemed too complicated. (*Slight pause.*)

Milly But surely it's quite straightforward. Surely what you mean is the first time he rang you answered and he asked for Marijke and you asked him who it was, but he went on speaking presumably and took no notice of what you said.⌐ It seems quite straightforward to me. ⌐ Isn't that what happened, Frank?⌐ Because really I don't

248

see why he couldn't just've said that in the first place, why he couldn't just've said: Michael rang but he couldn't hear me, or words to that effect.

Frank ⌈You mean Alec.

Milly I said Alec.

Frank You said Mike.

Milly Well I meant Alec.⌋ Obviously I meant Alec.

Pause. Marijke audible.

Do you know I'd love to visit the bulbs. Because we'd set our hearts on seeing the bulbs and then we saw that programme about the drugs, didn't we Frank. And of course it put me right off the bulbs because the drugs are terrible over there. You can buy drugs in the shops, can't you Frank, just walk in and buy them.

Pause. Marijke audible.

Milly It put me right off.

Silence. Faint ping of receiver replaced.

(*Calls.*) Marijke. (*Slight pause.*) Marijke. (*Slight pause.*) (*Normal voice.*) Marijke, what's the name of the place Frank and I almost went to? (*Slight pause.*)

Marijke (*from the doorway throughout*) Do you mean the *Keukenhof* gardens?

Milly That's right. The Cookenhoff. It sounds so odd the way she says it. It doesn't sound like the sort of place you'd expect bulbs somehow. (*Slight pause.*) Was that Alec?

Marijke I'm sorry, Mrs Taylor?

Milly Frank said poor Alec was having trouble with the phone.

Marijke I'm sorry?

Milly ⌈It was Alec you said, wasn't it Frank?

Frank I thought it was Alec.⌋

Milly He thought it was Alec. Wasn't it Alec?

Pause.

Marijke Alec is in Israel, Mrs Taylor.

Milly Well no wonder he had trouble getting through. ⌈ No wonder he had trouble, Frank.⌋ Is he having nice weather over there?

Marijke He has been away all summer. In the kibbutz.

Milly He must think a lot of you to phone from all that way.

Marijke I'm sorry?

Frank ⌈Marijke's saying it wasn't Alec,⌋ aren't you Marijke.

Milly ⌈But she's saying he rang. He just rang.

Frank I don't think he did.

Milly What do you mean you don't think he did? Marijke just said he did.

Frank Marijke said he's in Israel.

Milly I know he's in Israel. He's been there all summer in a kibbutz, I'm not deaf, Frank.

Frank He didn't ring.

Milly You mean he couldn't get through.

Frank I mean he didn't try.

Milly But you spoke to him, Frank.

Frank I was wrong.

Milly You told me you'd spoken to him.⌋

Pause.

Well who was it then if it wasn't Alec? You know you
really don't have to be so secretive about your boyfriends,
Marijke. Marijke. Marijke, please don't walk off while
I'm speaking. (*Slight pause.*) I say you really don't have
to be so secretive about your boyfriends. Because Frank
and I would like to meet your friends more often,
wouldn't we Frank. Because of course we know Alec by
sight and I've always said to Frank he looks like a very
nice boy but do you know I can't remember when we
last spoke to him. ⌈Can you Frank.⌋ Except on the
phone.

Pause.

Marijke Which meat am I to put out, Mrs Taylor?

Milly Which meat?

Marijke Last night you said remember to put out the
frozen meat.

Milly Didn't I say lamb? I thought I'd said lamb.

Marijke Which is the lamb?

Milly Isn't it labelled?

Marijke I couldn't see lamb.

Milly Chops. It should be labelled chops.

Slight pause.

Marijke Chops.

Milly Do you want me to come, Marijke? (*Slight pause.*)
I won't be a moment.

Silence as Marijke and Milly go.

251

Frank (*relaxed and rambling*) The more I think about it . . . the more certain I am . . . that it was the Bahamas. Because of course that was the year Marijke. Why did I say Marijke. I mean Irene. That was the year Irene lost her child. Do you know they came back and the house had been ransacked. They knew exactly what they wanted. Jewellery. Electricals. And of course they had all the time in the world. (*Pause.*) No I can't imagine why Mill has such a bee in her bonnet about the Canaries. (*Pause.*) Of course it broke her heart.

    Pause.

Naturally you can't entirely rule out the sexual motive because after all there's no doubt that Irene is a very attractive woman, a very attractive woman. But I do think Mill makes rather too much of a meal of it. Because I've been into it in some detail, and if as Irene says this black chappie followed her from the bank, then it does seem reasonable to assume doesn't it that his motive was a financial one. Although who's to say that at the back of his mind like any man he wasn't aware of the further possibilities so to speak. (*Pause. Faint laugh.*) Some of the girls he used to bring back when he was still living at home, they were quite extraordinary. In fact we've often said Irene's quite a plain Jane compared to some of those girls. We used to ask ourselves: where on earth did he find so much charm. And then to see him with Irene. Why did I say Irene. I mean Marijke. To see him with Marijke. Who must be what half his age at least. I mean at most, don't I. Half his age at the most. To see the two of them you'd think he was still a boy himself the way they were carrying on. (*Faint laugh.*) Those tulips . . . (*Faint laugh.*)

Milly (*entering room*) He's not talking about that dog again is he. [Really Frank don't you think we've all had enough of that dog for one day.

Pause.

Frank Any joy?

Milly Any joy, Frank?

Frank Did you have any joy with the chops?⌋

Milly You know sometimes I think Marijke inhabits an entirely different world to the rest of us. ⌈She wasn't even looking in the right freezer, Frank.⌋ But I suppose I mustn't complain. Because young people make all the difference to a house. That's why I say: we'd like to see her friends more. But of course it's a secretive age. I suppose I was secretive about Frank when I was her age. Although I really can't imagine why. It's not as if we had anything to hide. Because our pleasures were quite innocent in those days. In those days we just hadn't heard of sex and drugs.

Frank ⌈We'd heard of sex, Mill.⌋

Milly Well yes we'd heard of it. But it wasn't being rammed down your throat all the time, that's my point. And as for drugs.

Frank Marijke wouldn't take drugs.

Milly Well of course Marijke wouldn't take drugs. ⌈But if Frank will let me finish what I was going to say,⌋ what I was going to say was what sort of a world is it where you can just walk into a shop and buy them that's what I'd like to know.

Pause.

Frank Alec seems a nice enough lad though.

Milly Oh yes, I've no objections to Alec. I can't say I like his stud, naturally. But I'm sure he'll grow out of it.

Frank ⌈His stud?⌋

Milly I realise they're all the rage.

Frank ⌈I didn't know he had a stud, Mill.

Milly He's always had a stud, Frank.⌋ Yes he's always had a stud. For as long as we've known him. And it's not something I'd take issue with. I assume he's aware of the risks.

Frank Do you know I'd no idea he had a stud.

Milly Because it can't be hygienic to have something like that in your nose. I know I'd've died if Michael had come home with something like that in his nose, wouldn't I Frank. We're so lucky he never rebelled.

Frank I wouldn't say he never rebelled.

Milly ⌈Wouldn't you?⌋

Pause.

Frank It wouldn't be honest to say we'd never had our difficult moments with Mike.

Milly Oh yes we've had our difficult moments. ⌈But he was never a rebel, Frank. He never disfigured himself.⌋ He was always clean. I'm not saying Alec isn't clean, but Michael always looked it.

Frank He had a guitar.

Milly Yes, but he never played it.

Frank It was quite an expensive guitar.

Milly And he was always polite. He wouldn't be where he is today if he wasn't polite to clients.

Pause.

Frank It was quite an expensive guitar. ⌈What was the name of it, Mill?⌋ It was Japanese, but it didn't sound it.

Milly Because whenever he brought a girl home for example, he'd always introduce her. [Didn't he Frank.]

Frank I remember being quite surprised to discover it was made in Japan.

Milly [I said didn't he Frank.

Slight pause.

Frank Didn't he what?]

Slight pause.

Milly Some of those girls . . . (*With increasing tension.*) Of course I don't mean in any way to disparage Irene, because I'm sure she's a very attractive woman, very attractive, in her way. But the fact remains Irene was really quite the plain Jane compared to some of those girls. And he's never lost his charm, Michael. We often used to ask ourselves where he got it from, that charm of his. Because it didn't come from Frank, did it Frank. And I don't mean to say it was wasted on Irene. Of course not. Because clearly Irene had something the others didn't. Or Michael felt she had at least. And it's not up to us to question his judgement, is it Frank.

Pause.

Frank Mill was very upset by the operation.

Milly It was coming out of the blue like that.

Frank Mill was surprised they didn't mention it beforehand.

Milly They could've at least mentioned it. (*Pause.*) And the thing is we still don't really know why, do we Frank.

Frank [Well we think we might know why.]

Milly Well yes we think we might know why, but we might be wrong.

Frank But clearly she'd made up her mind she didn't want children.

Milly (*raising voice*) Yes but there are ways and means, Frank. There are ways and means.

Long silence.

Frank I've said to Mill, perhaps next year we'll manage to get away. Next year when Marijke's gone. ⌈Haven't I Mill.⌋ Oh it won't be anywhere very grand. It won't be Tenerife. (*Pause. Jovial.*) ⌈I say it won't be Tenerife, will it Mill.⌋ (*Pause.*) We've been looking through some brochures already. That's where we saw the Dutch weekend as a matter of fact. We thought the Dutch weekend was very good value. Because the price included the tour to the bulbs, didn't it Mill, and it's not often the price includes the organised tours these days.

Pause.

Milly (*softly*) ⌈We would never've dared do that, would we Frank.

Frank Dared do what, Mill?

Milly Walk off. Walk off like that while somebody was speaking.⌋

Pause.

Frank We could manage Spain. I've said to Mill we could probably manage Spain.

Milly I've told Frank he can forget Spain.

Frank There are some very attractive offers if you go at the right time.

Milly ⌈I'm not going to Spain, Frank.⌋

Frank Mike's been out there. He says it's not at all what you'd imagine.

Milly ⌈I really don't care who's been out there, Frank.⌋
I've told Frank I really don't care what Michael says
because the fact is you're likely to be attacked. I've
spoken to people who've been attacked.

Frank ⌈I didn't know that.⌋

Milly Joan was attacked only recently. That was Spain.

Frank ⌈Whereabouts?

Milly Spain. Somewhere in Spain.⌋ She said the people –
the Spaniards or whatever they are – she said they just
stood and watched. And then of course no one spoke a
word of English did they. She said at the police station
they just jabbered away it was quite disgraceful. That
was Spain. The man who did it had a gun. She told the
police she'd seen a gun, but they took no notice, she
could've been shot for all they cared. And of course now
she's home she's moved heaven and earth to get her
money back, but do you know the agents claim they're
not responsible for what happened. Not responsible. Can
you imagine?

Frank ⌈Whereabouts was that, Mill?

Milly Spain, Frank. I've told you: it was Spain.⌋
Sometimes I wonder if he's listening to a word I'm
saying.

Frank Well of course I'm listening to what Mill says
about the violence over there, but there's also violence
over here.

Milly Well I know there's violence over here but it's not
the same violence because their attitude to women is
completely different ⌈that's my point Frank. And if you
remember⌋ we decided that although the price of the
Dutch weekend included the tour of the bulbs the fact
was, that particular Dutch weekend which included the

tour of the bulbs was the most expensive Dutch weekend we looked at.

Pause.

Heaven and earth she's moved.

Pause.

Do you know sometimes I say to Frank, don't I Frank, I say sometimes I think I'd be quite happy if I never went anywhere. Because of course the Cookenhoff or whatever it's called looks very attractive, but then we do have flowers here. It's not as if we don't have flowers here.

Pause.

(*Softly.*) We were sitting by the pool. That man made such a nice job of the pool. And I'd noticed that Irene was looking rather haggard because I'd said to Frank hadn't I Frank don't you think Irene's looking rather haggard, because of course it's not like Irene to look like that she usually looks so gay. (*Slight pause.*) And even then I had to worm it out of her didn't I Frank, and if I hadn't do you know I still think we'd be sitting here in ignorance because that's the thing that really upsets us isn't it Frank, that it's quite clear if I hadn't wormed it out neither of them had any intention of telling us. We'd still've been sitting here in ignorance, wouldn't we Frank. (*Slight pause.*) She said she'd made up her mind, I said yes Irene it's quite obvious you've made up your mind, but surely there are ways and means I mean it's such a step to've taken, because after all you're still an attractive young woman with your whole life ahead of you or the greater part of it at any rate. (*Slight pause.*) She said there's hardly any scar, not that you'd notice. And that was the end of the subject ⌈wasn't it Frank. Frank. (*Louder.*) Frank. (*Slight pause.*) I say: that was the end of the subject wasn't it.⌋

Long silence.

Marijke (*from the doorway*) Excuse me, Mrs Taylor.

Milly Yes? Yes what is it Marijke? (*Slight pause.*) ⌈ Flowers Frank.⌋ That was a nice thought.

Marijke The stems had snapped.

Milly Those cats. ⌈Look Frank. Wasn't that a nice thought of Marijke's.⌋

Marijke Where shall I put them?

Milly We'll have them in here I think. Yes this room could do with some colour. (*Slight pause.*) Those cats. I've said to Frank I'm sure there's something you can buy, I'm sure there's something you can put down. (*Pause. Faint laugh.*) You know it reminds me of those tulips. Frank and I were just saying about those tulips, Marijke. Because it was such a funny idea, wasn't it. ⌈ Wasn't it Frank.⌋

With mounting amusement as before:.

Frank Mike can be a real comedian when he wants to be.

Milly It took her quite by surprise, didn't it Frank. Because you see she was curled up on the sofa reading a book, weren't you Marijke, and Michael sneaked in, and the next thing you know they were both in fits, weren't they Frank . . . (*She begins to laugh.*)

Frank I really didn't think that old sofa would be able to take it . . . (*He begins to laugh.*)

Milly I don't even think they realised we were all watching, the state they were in, but of course someone had left the dining-room hatch open . . .

Frank Mill said to me, where's the camera . . .

Milly But of course he doesn't have a flash . . . And what was it you said to him, Marijke? ⌈What was it she said to Michael, Frank?⌋

Frank It was something like, what am I supposed to do with them . . .

Milly That's right . . . What am I supposed to do with them. And so Michael said . . . ⌈What did he say to her, Frank?⌋ . . .

Frank (*laughing more*) It wasn't so much what he said . . . It was the way he said it . . .

Milly (*laughing more*) What was it he said, Marijke? . . . Of course we were all in hysterics by this time, you can imagine. Even Irene had to laugh. What was it he said? . . .

Marijke (*now inside the room*) I don't remember, Mrs Taylor.

Pause. Frank and Milly continue to laugh.

I don't remember his exact words.

Pause. Frank and Milly continue to laugh. Laughter ends.

Milly Oh dear . . . (*Faint after-laugh.*)

Silence.

Marijke (*with calm detachment throughout*) I don't remember the exact words he used. (*Slight pause.*) He came into the room silently and held the flowers between my face and the book. When I pushed them away he was laughing already and pushed them back again. Whenever I tried to move the book or the flowers he pushed them back in my face, laughing all the while. Everyone was laughing.

Pause.

Later that day when I mentioned I would be going swimming Mr Taylor said he would drive me. I said there was no need but he insisted he would drive me. I remember this clearly.

Pause.

I remember this clearly since it was in the car Mr Taylor invited me to stay with himself and his wife. He said wouldn't I like to swim in their pool in return for speaking *Afrikaansch* with him. I asked him why he should think I speak *Afrikaansch*. He said why not, isn't it Dutch? I explained I do not speak this kind of Dutch.

Pause.

A little further on he said do you know the *Walletjes* in *Amsterdam*? I replied yes I am familiar with the *Walletjes*, Mr Taylor. No doubt you have been as a tourist in *Amsterdam*. Because it is well known that tourists, first they tour the canals and historical buildings. Then, if it is the season, they visit the flowers in the *Keukenhof* gardens at Lisse. Or later in summer go to swim at *Zandvoort* or *Scheveningen*. And then when they are bored with the flowers and canals and the sea, then they will go to a live show perhaps or to the *Walletjes* to look at prostitutes in the shop windows there. It is a very popular tourist activity. I say certainly I know that area but it is not of particular interest to me. Mr Taylor says that surprises me.

Pause.

He says that surprises me *Marijke*, because you look like the sort of girl who would find it interesting.

Pause.

He says but of course I am right there is nothing so remarkable about prostitutes in shop windows. Mr Taylor says what interests him is rather when the window is empty and the lights are on in the back room. When the women are with their men-friends in other words. He says don't you find it interesting to think about what the women and their men-friends might be doing in those back rooms? I tell him I have never given much thought to the matter, but I should imagine it must be dull. He says that surprises me *Marijke*, because you don't look like the sort of girl who would find it dull.

Pause.

Some kilometres after this conversation Mr Taylor drives a little way off the road. He stops the car and shows me a little gun. We are on a kind of ridge with woodland behind, and ahead of us a steep fall into the valley. I ask him why have we stopped? He says why not stop, *Marijke*? This is a beautiful view. Don't you like the view? You won't find such views in your country. Your country's too flat. There's too much sky. Look down there at the shadows of the clouds.

Pause.

Mr Taylor asks me did I know a man had raped his wife. That's why he carries a gun, since a man has raped his wife. I say to him would it not be more appropriate, Mr Taylor, for your wife to carry the gun if that is the case. He says it's not funny *Marijke*, it's not a joke,

Pause. Faint laugh. Pause.

Then he asks me what do you wear in the baths, *Marijke*? I say what do you expect me to wear in the baths? He says are those your things in that bag. I say please Mr Taylor don't take my things out of the bag. He says but why not? What are you afraid of? And for the first time I notice the look in his eyes.

Pause.

He takes my things from the bag and examines them
for a while in silence between his fingers. Then he says,
listen, shall we have a smoke? (*Slight pause.*) And when
I tell him I don't want to smoke with him he pushes the
things back and throws the bag in my face. He says
don't think I don't know your game. My wife was raped.
I know that game. I'm not a fool. I've known girls like
you, he says, plenty of girls like you.

Pause.

Later, in the afternoon, I have taken my book into the
garden. Mr Taylor comes and lies beside me. When I go to
move he takes hold of my arm. Don't go away *Marijke*,
he says. Can't you see my wife wants to take our
photograph. Mrs Taylor is standing with the camera
under the apple tree. Don't either of you move, she says.
Smile.

Long silence.

Milly Have you finished, Marijke? (*Pause.*) I say have
you finished with those flowers? (*Slight pause.*) Marijke.
(*Slight pause.*) Marijke, please don't walk off while I'm –

Silence as Marijke goes.

(*Faint laugh.*) [Look at those flowers, Frank. What on
earth has she been doing with them?]

Milly chuckles faintly. Frank joins in. Silence.

You know I really don't see that there was any need to
use that word. Do you? [Do you, Frank?]

Pause.

Frank I've been thinking . . . [I've been thinking, Mill,
You know I think you're right, it wasn't the Bahamas –

Milly Frank.

Frank Mill?

Pause.

Milly I say, I don't see what need there was to use that word.

Frank What word?

Milly The word she used.⌋ (*Slight pause.*) Because really Marijke's Dutch I mean her English is terribly good but still she has a very odd way of speaking sometimes to my mind, a very peculiar way of putting things. I'm sure she can't really mean to say half the things she says. (*Slight pause.*) Yes I'm surprised they haven't pulled her up on it, at the college. Because I've said to Frank, haven't I Frank, I've said I think they let the youngsters get away with too much these days. And Michael agrees with us. He says the trouble is too much freedom.

Pause.

⌈I didn't know he'd given her a lift, did you Frank?⌋ (*Slight pause.*) No I didn't realise he'd taken her for a spin, but of course it doesn't surprise me because as I say the two of them did hit it off rather well and Michael does like to drive. It's one of his great passions. He's had some lovely cars, hasn't he Frank. Well so has Irene. They've both had some lovely cars. ⌈What's the one you liked, Frank?⌋ There's one Frank particularly liked. ⌈ Which was it, Frank?⌋

Frank The BMW.

Milly That's right. I can remember Frank drooling over that BMW. (*Faint laugh. Slight pause.*) ⌈Frank. Are you alright Frank? You look a little peaky.⌋ He worries me when he goes pale like that. ⌈Don't you think you ought to go and lie down. No? What about your pills?⌋ (*Slight pause.*) He's such a worry sometimes, and the thing is all

his side of the family seem to die young, don't they
Frank.

Pause.

You know the more I hear about Holland the less I like
the sound of it.

Pause.

⌈What did she mean, Frank: smoke.⌋ Because Irene of
course has never been able to manage without a cigarette
in her mouth. But Michael . . . ⌈I've never see him smoke.
Have you Frank?⌋

Pause.

(*Faint laugh.*) You know that's so typical of Michael,
to say he'll drive someone somewhere, and then go
completely out of the way to look at the scenery. Because
of course he's got a head for business, he wouldn't be
where he is today if he didn't have a head for business,
but I've always said to Frank, haven't I Frank, I've
always said he's a romantic at heart. (*Faint laugh.*) The
shadows of clouds. (*Slight pause.*) Yes, he's like me in
that respect, the romantic respect. And of course that
was April. Because it's true we had some fine days in
April. But now look it's nearly the end of August and
it hasn't been what I'd call a summer at all. I'm sure
Marijke's legs must be terribly cold. It gives me the
shivers just to look at them. ⌈Doesn't it you, Frank.

Pause. Faint telephone audible as before.

Is that the phone, Frank?

Frank Shall I go?

Milly Won't Marijke go?⌋ More often than not it's for
Marijke these days.

Pause. Marijke audible on phone but unintelligible as before.

Milly Yes it's probably Alec or one of those.

Pause. Marijke audible.

(*Faint laugh.*) When Joan first saw him she said, what on earth has he got in his nose, Millicent? Is he a pig? (*Faint laugh.*) A pig. That's the thing about Joan, you can have a good laugh with her, can't you Frank. She sees the funny side. It's like a breath of fresh air. Even Spain, she says, is funny, in retrospect.

Pause. Marijke audible.

She's having a pool put in by the way. ⌈She's found a very reasonable man, Frank.⌋ She said after that experience she'd rather have her own. Oh it's nothing very luxurious. It certainly won't be heated. Just a basic pool. ⌈She said she'll let me have his number, Frank.⌋

Silence. Faint ping of receiver replaced.

Frank It was an Epiphone.

Milly ⌈Frank?

Frank That guitar of Mike's.⌋ I remember the name now. Because I remember thinking: it doesn't sound Japanese. Because it doesn't does it: Epiphone. But the man said it's all Japanese now. You won't find anything in *your* price range that isn't Japanese. (*Faint laugh.*)

Pause.

Milly Of course it's going to be very quiet without Marijke. When it's just the two of us again. Because we're used to her now, aren't we Frank. (*Slight pause.*) Oh yes we were wary at first. Naturally we were. Loud music. Boyfriends. Needless scenes. (*Slight pause.*) But

in fact it hasn't turned out at all like we'd imagined. [
Has it Frank.⌋

Pause.

Not that we worry about the quiet. In fact that's why we
came here, wasn't it Frank, for the quiet.

Frank [What's that?

Milly The quiet. I say that's why we came.⌋ Because I
said to Frank, didn't I Frank, I said really you know
these planes are driving us both up the wall. And then
we happened to see a programme, didn't we Frank,
about drugs, and of course that settled it.

Frank It was rats.

Milly Yes, rats. (*Slight pause.*) [What did I say, Frank?

Frank Drugs. You said drugs.

Milly Did I?⌋

Pause.

So when we arrived here of course the first thing we did
was go into the garden. [I'm sure I said rats, Frank.⌋
Because it was the most glorious summer then. And
Frank took my arm and we stood for a moment under
the apple tree to be out of the heat. All that fruit. I said
heavens Frank, what are we going to do with all that
fruit, just the two of us. And he said to me don't worry
about that Mill, listen. Didn't you Frank. And I said
what do you mean Frank, listen. And he said, nothing,
just listen.

Long silence.

IN THE REPUBLIC OF HAPPINESS

an entertainment in three parts

1 DESTRUCTION OF THE FAMILY

2 THE FIVE ESSENTIAL FREEDOMS
OF THE INDIVIDUAL

3 IN THE REPUBLIC OF HAPPINESS

In the Republic of Happiness was first performed at the Royal Court Jerwood Theatre Downstairs, London, on 6 December 2012.

Mum / Middle-Aged Woman Emma Fielding
Hazel / Teenage Girl 2 Ellie Kendrick
Granny / Old Woman Anna Calder-Marshall
Grandad / Old Man Peter Wight
Dad / Middle-Aged Man Stuart McQuarrie
Uncle Bob / Man of about Thirty Paul Ready
Madeleine / Woman of about Thirty Michelle Terry

Director Dominic Cooke
Set Designer Miriam Buether
Costume Designer Moritz Junge
Lighting Designer Peter Mumford
Composer Roald van Oosten
Sound Designer Paul Arditti
Musical Director James Fortune
Casting Director Amy Ball
Assistant Director Adele Thomas
Assistant Designer Lucy Sierra
Production Managers Paul Handley, Tariq Rifaat

Characters

Eight actors are required, as follows

PART ONE	PART TWO	PART THREE
Grandad	**Old Man**	
Granny	**Old Woman**	
Dad	**Middle-Aged Man**	
Mum	**Middle-Aged Woman**	
Debbie	**Teenage Girl 1**	
Hazel	**Teenage Girl 2**	
Madeleine	**Woman** of about thirty	**Madeleine**
Uncle Bob	**Man** of about thirty	**Uncle Bob**

· *Assignment of roles*

In Parts One and Three
roles are assigned in the usual way.

In Part Two
there are no assigned parts,
and the whole company should participate.

A dash before a speech —
indicates change of speaker.

DESTRUCTION OF THE FAMILY

Daylight. Christmas.

A small artificial tree with lights.

The family is gathered: Mum, Dad, Granny, Grandad, Debbie, Hazel.

Dad stares at Debbie. Silence.

Debbie I wasn't trying to upset people, Dad. I love you. And I love Mum. Plus I love Granny and Grandad – and of course I love Hazel too. I do, Hazel – whatever you think. But the fact is, is I know that I'll love my baby more. And that's how it should be, Dad – however much I love you, I know that I'll love my baby more. Which is why I'm afraid. Wouldn't you be afraid? When you look at the world? – when you imagine the future? I'm afraid, Dad – for my baby. And I'm really sorry because I know this is Christmas and I shouldn't be talking like this about horrible things but it's just I can't help it.

Mum You mustn't apologise, Debs. Tommy's not really angry – are you, Tom.

Hazel So why doesn't she just get rid of it?

Mum Hazel doesn't mean that.

Hazel Yes I do – if the world isn't 'good enough'.

Granny That's not a nice thing to say, Hazel.

Mum She doesn't actually mean it.

Hazel Yes I do.

  Pause.

Mum So you went to the supermarket, Margaret.

Granny Oh it's not very interesting.

Mum *We* think it's interesting. What did you get? Come on – tell us – cheer us all up.

Granny Well – I bought a lettuce –

Mum Really?

Granny Yes.

Mum A nice one?

Granny Yes quite a nice lettuce, and a packet of biscuits.

Mum Wonderful!

Granny Oh and some material for your Grandad.

Debbie Material? What kind of / material?

Hazel She means pornography. (*To Grandad.*) Why don't you just get it off the internet, Grandad?

Granny He's frightened someone will steal his identity, Hazel – and anyway it's always much nicer having the actual magazine.

Mum Well I'm very sorry but I think that's wrong. I wouldn't buy pornography for Tommy.

Debbie Please stop it, Mum – why 're you trying to make Grandad feel guilty? It's not as if he's going to *do* anything – he just likes looking – looking's not a crime.

Grandad Don't you talk about me like that, young lady. I am neither senile nor impotent – surprising as that may seem.

Debbie Sorry, Grandad – in fact I was defending you – but in future I'll keep my mouth shut. Okay?

Pause.

Granny Where're all the light bulbs, Tom?

Mum What's wrong, Margaret?

Granny What's happened to all the light bulbs? There's none in the toilet and I'm just looking and it looks to me like there are none in here either.

Hazel It's because electricity's got so expensive, Granny.

Granny Well yes – I know electricity's expensive but eventually it will get dark. What happens when it gets too dark to see?

Hazel We get the box out of course.

Granny What box?

Mum The box with the light bulbs in – don't we, Tommy.

Pause.

Tommy? Is something the matter?

Dad D'you think this bird's been properly cooked?

Mum Why 're you asking me that?

Dad It's just that ever since we started this meal I've felt a bit sick.

Granny You can't 've done, Tom – of course it's cooked – it's delicious, Sandra.

Mum Thank you.

Granny Exceptionally succulent.

Mum Thank you.

Granny Which part did you stuff?

Mum The neck.

Granny Because you know not to stuff the body.

Mum Of course not: I stuffed the neck.

Granny Don't stuff the body – it won't cook.

Mum I didn't.

Granny You're sure? Because these bacteria can be very /
dangerous.

Mum I know what I've stuffed.

Granny Well anyway, I think it's excellent.

Mum Thank you.

Dad Then why does my mouth taste of vomit?

Granny It can't be the bird, Tom.

Dad Well in that case it must be my particularly selfish
daughter bringing up yet again the subject of her
unplanned and ill-conceived pregnancy in front of this
whole family when *she can't even name the father*.

Debbie I'm sorry, Dad.

Mum Don't bang on the table like that.

Dad I'll bang how the fuck I like.

    Pause.

Granny He's been like this ever since he was little.
People don't change. But he does need to control his
temper – especially at Christmas.

Dad Yes, Mum – okay – I take your point – I'm sorry.

Granny People don't change – you learn that when you
get to my age.

Hazel But you've changed, Granny.

Granny I don't think so. How?

Hazel You used to be young and pretty.

Mum Hazel.

Hazel Well it's true: people don't change is rubbish.

Granny And what did Santa bring you for Christmas, Debbie?

Debbie Well I can't honestly go asking for presents when I've already got the most marvellous gift of all.

Hazel Lying cow – I saw the list!

Debbie What list?

Hazel She made this long long list of all the things she wanted – and because she's pregnant she got them.

Mum Please. Hazel.

Hazel The hat – the radio – the car – the 'nice little diamond earrings'.

Debbie I need a car to get to the hospital for my scans – and anyway you got that dress.

Hazel Why doesn't she use the bus? Granny's old and she uses the bus. So what if I got a dress – big deal – it wasn't exactly expensive.

Dad Mum? – on a bus? – you're joking – when did you last get on a bus, Mum?

Mum Leave your poor mother alone, Tommy.

Granny No he's right – because in fact, Hazel, your father is right, I don't use the bus, I take taxis. I may be an ugly old granny – as you have so kindly pointed out – but I still like to sit in the back of a taxi and be driven through the streets – especially at dusk in summer with all the smells of plants and restaurants coming in through the window – and all the childless young people in light summer clothes swarming on the pavements outside the shops and bars. I like to watch the meter running. I like to think ah these two minutes in a taxi have already cost me what that man emptying the bins will take more than an hour of his life to earn – and oh the extra stink of a rubbish bin in summer! Yes on nights like that the taxi is glorious and the fact I'm paying for my happiness makes my happiness all the sweeter – and the fact that other people are having to suffer and work just to pay for such basic things as electricity makes it even sweeter still. And when I'm cruising the clogged streets watching all those people your age, Hazel, all those childless and carefree people swarming outside the bars like ants outside of an ant-hole, I sometimes wonder if we are not on the verge of some enormous and magnificent change – don't you think? Yes I mean a change to our actual human material. Compared to which your sister's pregnancy – unplanned and ill-conceived as it may well be, plus medicalised beyond all reason by those same profitable concerns who have so often flown me (oh I admit it) to conferences and booked me into comfy hotel rooms – compared to which reproduction of your sister's kind – involving some kind of man, some kind of penetration, and even perhaps (I'm just guessing now, Debbie) some kind of wide-eyed love – might only be capable of churning out more of the same – more and more of exactly the same – and is that what we really want? Because what I'm imagining – Hazel – in that taxi of mine, is a new kind of magnificent human being who may not even be human at all.

Hazel Well I still don't see why she needs a car.

Mum The thing is Hazel sweetheart is that's not for you to decide. And just because Debbie puts something on her list it doesn't mean she automatically gets it.

Hazel She got the car.

Mum She needs the car to go to the hospital.

Hazel And I suppose she needs those earrings to go to the hospital too.

Debbie storms out.

Mum Please don't leave the table – please – please don't storm off like that – she doesn't mean it.

Hazel Well I'm sorry but I think the way you're both spoiling her is horrible.

Pause.

Dad Very interesting, Mum – what you just said.

Granny Oh I know you think I'm an idiot, Tom.

Dad Not at all, not at all.

Mum Look I know I'm just your mother, Hazel. And I know that means I'll shop and cook and clean for you for ever and ever. You'll come home from your second failed marriage just like I'm sure you'll come home from your first just like you used to from school trips with a big bag full of dirty washing and expecting your dinner. And that's fine. If you can't make a marriage work, that won't be your fault. I agree that men with their fat thighs and their legs apart on trains can be impossible and that unselfish and faithful men like Daddy, or like Grandad here, are the exception, not the rule. Yes, I'm just your mother, and as such I expect to be trodden on and trodden on – I expect to be worn away like a stone step – and I'm prepared – like the stone – to endure it. But that doesn't mean I've no feelings, Hazel. My heart isn't stone too.

Hazel I'll go and talk to her.

Mum Thank you.

Hazel goes.

Are you alright there, Terry? Would you like some more meat?

Grandad Because I am neither senile, I'll have you know, nor impotent. – Just a little, please. – I won't be put down and I won't be put into a home. There are all kinds of erections – an erection doesn't have to be rock hard – it can still be useful. I never locked him in a cellar. I never abused you, Thomas – and I never abused your mother – not even when it was the fashionable thing. I've spent my whole life swimming against the tide. Well of course I had a mortgage, but I paid it off – nor do the police frighten me: I don't commit crimes – not serious ones – so don't think you can make me believe I'm losing my memory then shut me away in a home. I've paid my way – there's money in the bank and I'll spend it however I like: I happen to enjoy ice creams and speedboat rides – that doesn't mean I'm a child or can be treated like one. Remember you're looking at a man who spent forty years in general practice and ten years before that in prison for a crime I never committed – so when men went into space, is it surprising I envied them their weightlessness? I wanted Tom to go into space – I'd hold him up when he was little and show him the moon – remember that, Tom? – remember those teddy-bear pyjamas? He could've walked on the moon – he needn't have spent his whole life processing planning-applications – but he had no spark – the moon was too far – he couldn't be bothered.

Dad is looking at him.

What?

Dad You were never in prison, Dad. You were never a doctor.

Grandad I never said I was, Tommy boy. I'm not stupid.

Mum Let's not start an argument.

Dad Why not? He loves it.

Mum was the doctor, Dad. Mum worked for forty years to support you. The reason you have money in the bank now for speedboat rides and pornographic downloads is that while you squandered, Mum constantly worked.

Granny He helped me in the house, Tom.

Dad Helped in the house? He can't even load a washing machine.

Granny You've no right / to insult him.

Dad Whatever. He can't hear me anyway.

Grandad Of course I can hear you: you're the one who's deaf.

Dad I may be going deaf – yes – but at least I have the intelligence to wear my hearing aid and actually switch it on.

Mum You're being cruel now.

Dad Correct.

Grandad What?

Dad Oh for godsake . . .

Grandad *What* did he say?

Dad I said correct, Dad – I am deaf – correct – you're right – you're absolutely right – forgive me.

Oh hello, what's this?

Debbie and Hazel have reappeared as perfect friends.

Friends now, are we?

Debbie Yes, Dad. Sorry.

Hazel No: it was my fault. I'm really sorry, Mum. I've been a complete cunt.

Mum Well as long as you're friends now.

Granny What's going on, girls?

Debbie We're going to sing for you, Granny.

Mum Sing?

Hazel We want to sing for you all like we did when we were little.

Mum Well that's wonderful!

Dad Is it something we know?

Debbie It's something we both made up.

Debbie and Hazel sing.

Debbie / Hazel

> We're going to marry a man
> (going to marry a man)
> The man will be rich
> The man will say bitch:
>> I'll make him pay for my meals
>> I'll strut and fuck him in heels –
> That's our incredible plan
> Yes our incredible plan.
>
> We're going to carry a gun
> (going to carry a gun)
> The gun will go bang
> and puncture the man:
>> I'll aim my gun at his head
>> I'll pump his balls up with lead –
> Oh what incredible fun
> Yes what incredible fun.
>
> We're going to sharpen a knife
> (going to sharpen a knife)
> The knife will be real
> The blade will be steel:

I'll cut my name in his thighs –
cut out his tongue if he lies –
That's how to be a good wife
Yes how to be a good wife.

We'll send our man to the moon
(send our man to the moon)
The moonlight will shine
on your man and mine –
I'll keep his rocket on track
I'll make him radio back:
Oh darling marry me soon
(yes darling – marry me –
oh marry me soon)

*Enter from the background where he has silently
appeared: Uncle Bob.*
*Uncle Bob wears distinctive clothes, perhaps a well-
pressed polo shirt and brand-new jogging pants.*
Uncle Bob claps.

Uncle Bob Marvellous – marvellous singing, girls.

Girls Uncle Bob! Uncle Bob!

Uncle Bob Girls! Hello! Sandra! Tommy! Margaret!
Happy Christmas!

Girls Happy Christmas! Happy Christmas, Uncle Bob!

Some of the others also murmur 'Happy Christmas'.

Uncle Bob Marvellous – what a marvellous song.

Mum What're you doing here, Robert?

Uncle Bob Well to be frank with you, I've really no idea.
I thought I would just suddenly appear, so I did. I suddenly
appeared. I craved your company – craved to be with
you all – and here I am. I hope I'm not putting you out
at all.

Dad Of course not – you're very welcome.

Mum Girls – fetch Robert a chair.

Uncle Bob Oh no no no no no – no chair for me – I can't stay.

Granny You've only just arrived.

Uncle Bob I still can't stay.

Hazel Please – please stay – why can't you?

Debbie Please make him stay, Mum.

Uncle Bob Listen – I'd love to stay. You think I don't want to? Of course I want to. What a marvellous warm house, and what a great great welcome you've all given me. There are so many reasons to stay here – and all of them really persuasive: the smell of roast meat – red wine – the crackling log fire* – these two lovely girls with their whole lives ahead of them – and even – if my instincts are right – and they usually are – they usually always are – even – in beautiful young Debbie's case – yes look – the promise – and how appropriate to the time of year! – the radiant promise of new life to come. *Plus* there's the joy of seeing my sister again – how are you, Sandra? don't look so scared of me, I'm fine – and of being – thanks to her marriage to Tom here – can I call you Tom, Tommy? Or do you prefer Thomas? – I'm not sure he can hear me – anyway, of being, thanks to your marriage to Thomas, Tom, whatever, part now of this marvellous family. Because I am, yes, part now of this family, among whom – if that's not too formal of me – I number this lady Margaret – Peg, as I think you like to be known – yes: Doctor Peg and Terry here – happy Christmas, Terry – number these two human beings Terry and Peg among my most valued friends – and I am

---

* There is no crackling log fire.

perfectly sincere about that, even though I can see from your eyes – Terry – that you don't necessarily believe me – which is a shame.

Mum What is it you want, Robert?

Uncle Bob One moment, big sister, I'm still talking to Terry.

Debbie Grandad's not been well.

Uncle Bob I'm sorry to hear that, Debbie – but your grandad still needs to understand that when I say I value him as I friend, I mean it. Because I do mean it, Terry. I'm not someone who can say what they don't mean – understood?

Grandad makes gesture of friendly agreement.

Excellent. So – anyway – as I've said – there're a number of very persuasive reasons to stay here and make myself comfortable on the chair that young Deborah – are those real diamonds, sweetheart? – has got out for me – lovely: can I touch? –

She allows him to touch her ears.

Beautiful – really beautiful – yes really persuasive reasons to stay –

Debbie You're hurting me.

Uncle Bob What?

Debbie You're hurting me.

Uncle Bob I'm sorry – did that pinch? – I wish I could – yes really wish that I could but I can't. I want to but I can't. Did I hurt you? Sorry.

Granny What is it you're trying to say to us, Robert?

Uncle Bob Exactly, Peg – good question. Let me answer it.

Dad Is he staying or not?

Mum I don't know, Tom.

Uncle Bob Okay. Okay. It's like this.

We're on our way to the airport. Madeleine, I mean,
and myself. We're leaving. We're leaving the country
now. We won't be coming back. We've reached a decision
and it's irreversible. Why? Don't ask. Don't even ask.
We're going and that's that. You won't see us ever again.
You won't see me, you won't see Madeleine. That's why
she's asked me to come in now. Because basically this is
the only opportunity she has – before we both leave –
before we both irreversibly vanish – for her to tell you
how much she hates you – yes hates you and abhors this
family.

Now look – obviously – obviously I would much
rather she told you this herself. I said to her: something
like that, Madeleine, you've got to tell them yourself –
not me. But Madeleine points out that she can't. And it's
true: she quite honestly can't. There simply aren't the
hours in the day. Her workload's appalling. And in fact
she's doing her messages now – out there in the car – I
know: on Christmas Day – unfair – incredible – but that's
the kind of life she leads – now – do it – can't not – how
can she not? – because once we're on that plane it's total
dead time – hours of nothing – temazepam then nothing –
total dead time till we land – and even then . . . even
then . . . Well anyway – what was I saying? – oh yes,
about Madeleine – about what she would like me to say
to you.

Any chance of a glass of water?
And actually yes I think I will sit down for a moment.

Hazel brings him a glass of water.

Thank you, Hazel. Nice dress. Is it new? I like this –
what d'you call this?

He takes the fabric of her short skirt between his fingers.

Hazel The hem?

Uncle Bob The hem – of course it is – lovely.

He toys with the hem of the dress while he drinks the water.

Grandad Ten years.

Uncle Bob What's that, Terry?

Grandad Ten years for a crime I didn't commit.

Uncle Bob I know. Horrible.

(*Softer and more intense.*) But look: this is not me speaking now, it's Madeleine. She hates you. She finds each one of you in your own way abhorrent. But it's deeper than that, it's deeper than that, it goes much deeper than that because it affects her physically – affects her skin – so even now – out there in the car – she's having to rub in cream. She abreacts. You're actually affecting – yes – fact – her ability to breathe. And it's you, Peg, it's you and Terry – okay, let's start there – because you're both so old, she hates you. Okay? She hates this   this   this smell you have – she says you both smell like flood-damaged carpet and wishes you were dead. Horrid. I know. And not just dead but wants to erase you. I wish I could select them – is what she in fact says – and click delete – I want – yes – to permanently delete not just them but each of their cells, each memory. What do I care about the little shops where they bought sweets, the old currencies they still think in? So what if Peg age five cut her knee skipping and still has the scar – and if Terry remembers the clatter of horse-drawn traps or the signalman shutting by hand the level-crossing gate, so fucking what, so fucking what, she says. This idea that an old person somehow distils life's essence like a what? like an oil refinery? she totally refutes. She totally refutes, Peg, *plus* there's the cost, there's the unreasonable cost – Terry – of keeping somebody like yourself alive. Why?   Why?   Why – says Madeleine – are we bothering? And please: it's not me saying this, it's her – yes, why do we bother with that old fool? Look at his life – a succession of failures – one business crashing after the other: tropical forestry – mail-order cat-accessories – then there were the pre-booked trips – am I right? – into space, for which you went on taking the clients' money long after the whole doomed project / had been scrapped.

Grandad Not all of them failed.

Debbie Leave him alone.

Uncle Bob Yes they did fail, Terry – all of them failed – and please don't interrupt me, sweetheart, because I have a plane to catch and what I am trying to say is long, is very very long and difficult to remember – yes they did fail. They did. And when poor Madeleine thinks about that life of failure crowned now by your mental collapse I am to tell you she doesn't just want to scream she wants to drink acid.

Mum Robert?

Uncle Bob What? – (*Inward.*) But it's deeper than that, it's deeper than that – wants to drink acid but it goes much deeper than that –
  What?

Mum I think you should leave.

Uncle Bob You think I don't *want* to leave? You think I get *pleasure* from having to stay here and repeat what another person has instructed me to say? You think this doesn't *hurt*? Because I'm afraid she's right, Sandra: this is so typical of you – so typical of you and Tom in your

what? in your yes in your married bubble of stale air not
to understand how your own brother could be suffering
right now – yes? – yes? – look at me – yes?

I mean you've probably never seen the skin here, have
you – Madeleine's skin – here – between her armpit and
her breast – you've never seen it like I have, not felt with
your own fingertips have you Tom the horrid rash she
gets here when she considers your marriage. You've
probably never run your hand like I have along the inside
of her thigh have you Tom where hard lumps erupt
between her legs when she considers your marriage.

It disgusts her, Tom. I'm sorry. I can't not say it. She
insists I say it. It's the love. It's the long long terrifying
years of love. I am instructed to tell you that those long
years of love have burnt up – yes, this is right – have
burnt up all the oxygen and what's left is a vacuum.
They don't even hear my voice – she says – because
there's no air left for it to travel through. House – job –
school – kids – family – they don't even hear my voice –
and their ready-made opinions switch on like the security
lights protecting their property and illuminate the same
blank space . . . (*He loses the thread.*) The same blank
space . . . blank space . . . the same / blank space . . .

Dad You should calm down, Bobby boy. Have a drink –
come on – it's Christmas / – relax.

Uncle Bob . . . illuminate the same blank space and yes –
that's right – *if you will let me finish* – wants to take
your head, Sandra, between her two hands and bang it
against a wall – horrid, horrid – yes bang my own sister's
head – fact – repeatedly against a wall until what she
calls your   your   your   your *teeth* – yes –
break in your mouth. Now – as for the two girls – hmm –
as for the two girls . . . (*He loses the thread.*)

Debbie Uncle Bob?

293

Uncle Bob As for the two girls . . .

Hazel (*to Debbie*) This is all your / fault.

Uncle Bob As for the two girls . . .

Debbie (*to Hazel*) How is it mine / bitch?

Uncle Bob As for the two girls . . .

Debbie Uncle Bob – tell her it's not / my fault.

Uncle Bob As for the two – what?

Debbie Tell her this isn't / my fault.

Hazel Oh no nothing's ever your fault – little Miss 'I'm so pregnant / buy me a car'.

Uncle Bob As for the two girls . . . hmm . . .

Debbie I need to drive – tell her, Uncle Bob.

Uncle Bob What?

Debbie Tell her I need a car.

Uncle Bob What?

Debbie Tell Hazel I need to drive.

Granny Mums these days do need to drive a car, Robert – / Debbie's right.

Uncle Bob (*inward*) . . . but it's deeper than that, it's deeper than that, the whole thing / goes much deeper than that . . .

Grandad Not all of them failed, Peg – why did he say the space-rocket / thing failed?

Uncle Bob (*still more soft and intense*) Why were you ever born, Deborah?

Hazel Ha! – good question.

Uncle Bob She says: why were those two girls of theirs ever even born? – Horrid. – Wasn't there a test? she says. Why couldn't your sister screen them out? – Isn't that just the most horrible thing to say? – And when Madeleine thinks of your dividing and dividing cells glued to my sister's uterus, each with the same protein at its heart and now that same code of protein repeated and repeated inside young Debbie's mucus-plugged womb, she shakes me awake. Yes she shakes your poor Uncle Bob awake, girls, and bites right into me – can you imagine? And when I say bites I mean bites hard – draws blood. Then she passes her hand like this, girls, over my face – in the dark in bed, girls – like this – over your poor poor uncle's eyes and lips. And what she whispers is: that family – why were those girls of theirs ever even born? What're they supposed to find here on this earth? Trees? A cool stream? Do they really expect pear blossom to appear in spring? And now in wintertime – she says – when they have torn the wax strips from their legs in front of the crackling log fire – are they still expecting to hear the cheerful robin?

A long silence while he and the girls stare at each other. Finally:

Hazel Where does she bite you, Uncle Bob?

Mum Will somebody help me please with Grandad.

Uncle Bob (*reaching into pocket*) Ah – sorry – sorry – excuse me . . .

Two scenes develop at the same time: in the background, the family quietly and tenderly deal with Grandad, who has swallowed something the wrong way and started to cough. In the foreground, Uncle Bob answers his mobile phone while Hazel watches him.

Uncle Bob Yes hello?

Everything okay?

In the house – I'm still in the house.

I'm telling them now. It takes time, sweetheart.

I said it takes time – I'm not a machine.

I'm just saying I'm a human being not a machine: I can't can't – can't – whatever – I can't just –

I *know* when the plane leaves. I am fully aware of when the plane leaves, sweetheart – but we budgeted for that – don't you worry – the whole thing here is   is   is it's under control.

I'm sorry?

Why's that?

The *bathroom*? No. Listen to me: you can't –

You cannot come in here and use the bathroom, Madeleine. No.

(Shit. Fuck.)

Nothing – nothing – okay – whatever.

Love you too.

Mum That's it, Terry – just keep on coughing.

Dad What do we do, Mum – pat him on the back?

Granny You can try. Not too hard, though.

Dad Come on, Dad. Spit it out.

Granny Not too hard, Tom.

Mum Let's get him to stand up. Yes she's right: you're going to hurt him. Don't.

Debbie Come on, Grandad. We need you to stand up.

Granny If he's choking, he's choking – it won't make a difference standing him up.

Debbie (*getting him up*) That's it, Grandad. Cough it out. Are you better now? Maybe you want the bathroom?

Dad Would you like to use the bathroom, Dad? D'you want someone to wash your face?

Grandad starts to walk towards Uncle Bob.

Debbie You're going the wrong way, Grandad.

Uncle Bob ends call to find Grandad coming towards him. During the following, the light fades.

Uncle Bob Alright there, Terry?

Grandad I like hearing a man speak – but that's quite some mouth you've got.

Uncle Bob Oh?

Grandad Yes quite some mouth. (*With increasing authority and vehemence.*) I didn't spend the best years of my life in prison just so you can come here now today with that mouth of yours and poison me – and poison this family.
Proteins? I have them in my urine – so what? I choke on a piece of meat – sure – does that make me stupid? I exported to China. I exported to Vietnam. Steel. Rice. I felled whole forests and I dined with ambassadors. I dealt in antiquities. I mined for cobalt. I wore hand-made leather-soled boots and I paid for the laces in *hard cash*.
Flood-damaged carpet? Go to hell, Bobby boy. You don't smell so squeaky clean yourself.

A noise. Everyone except Grandad turns to look. Madeleine has entered and tripped over something on the floor. She looks like an ordinary and unassuming woman and carries a big soft bag.

Madeleine Bit dark in here.
Lost a shoe. (*She pulls her shoe back on.*)
Okay if I use the bathroom?

Mum Of course, Madeleine. You know where it is.

Madeleine Thanks.

Mum Lovely to see you.

Madeleine goes off with the bag. Pause.

(*Faint laugh.*) When did it get so dark?

What time is it, Tommy?

Dad I'm sorry, my love?

Mum The time: what time is it?

Dad The time?

Granny He's not switched on. Are you switched on, Tom?

Debbie Daddy?

Dad What?

Debbie What time is it?

Dad He's dropped his pills.

Granny Five past six, Sandra.

Dad You've dropped your pills, Dad. Help him please, Debbie.

Debbie Which ones are which?

Dad I've no idea. Just help him, would you.

Debbie kneels on the floor and starts collecting Grandad's pills.

Mum D'you think we should put the lights on? Someone's going to hurt themselves.

Dad We've got the tree.

Mum The tree's not very bright, Tom. I think we should get the bulbs out. Please? Can we?

Dad Okay.

Mum and Dad open a cardboard box with light bulbs packed in newspaper. They put them in various light fittings and switch them on.

Mum (*laughs*) Don't be so rude, Peggy.

Dad (*to Deb*) Careful with those: they're for his memory.

Mum What time's your flight, Robert?

Granny Has Madeleine put on weight?

Bob Don't think so, Peg. Why?

Granny She looks bulkier than I remember her.

Hazel Bulkier?

Granny Quite fat, yes.

Bob Madeleine's lost weight, as a matter of fact.

Hazel Do I look bulky, Uncle Bob?

Bob Mmm?

Hazel Have I got bulky thighs?

Bob I couldn't possibly comment, sweetheart.

Hazel (*to Debbie*) What am I doing?

Granny You know quite well what you're doing.

Bob (*to Mum*) Sorry?

Debbie goes on collecting Grandad's pills.

Debbie What're the pink ones for?

Grandad Can't remember. Sorry.

Debbie Can you stop her doing that, Mum.

Debbie (*to Hazel*) Flirting. It's horrible.

299

Hazel (*to Debbie*)
You can talk.

Mum I thought
you were on your
way to the airport.

Debbie Tell her
to stop, Mum.

Bob Yes we are –
we're on our way
to the airport
right now.

(*To Deb.*) I cannot
control your sister.

General pause as Mum and Dad light more lamps.

Grandad (*genial*)
What if it's
stillborn, Debs?

Debbie Please
don't say that,
Grandad.

Dad Dad – just
shut up now.

Grandad Keep
your hair on. It's
a legitimate
question.

General pause as Mum and Dad light more lamps.

Mum Does
Madeleine not have
a family?

Bob What's that?

I said: does
Madeleine not
have –

Hazel She asked
if Madeleine's got
a family.

Debbie That's all
of them, Grandad.

– exactly.

Dad (*to Mum*) **Bob** All of what?
Pass me another
forty [*watt bulb*] (*To Bob.*) His
would you. pills.

Granny (*smiles*)
Looking quite
bright now.

General pause as Mum and Dad complete final lamps.

Grandad We had
pears, didn't we
Mum You still Peg – *and* we
haven't answered had robins – we
my question. had a number of
Hazel Uncle Bob? robins – we gave
them all names
Bob What? and kept them in
Fine. Just ignore a shoebox.
me then. **Hazel** Mum asked
you a question.

Debbie Why did
you keep / robins
in a shoebox,
Grandad?

*Talking uninterruptedly from the moment she appears –
and totally transformed – Madeleine comes back in. She
has changed into a beautiful haute couture dress and
radiates charm, charisma, conviction, power.*

Madeleine I do   do   do   simply do not
believe it! All these lights just for me! How wonderful!
What wonderful lights! Tom! Thank you! Thank you!
Oh – oh – oh – but the looks on your faces! Whatever
has Robbie been telling you?! What've you *said* to them,
Robbie? I hope you haven't been being indiscreet?
Because this brother of yours, Sandra – and listen thank

301

you so much for letting me use your bathroom – can be horribly indiscreet. He cannot keep a single confidence to himself. *Plus* sexually too – well can you, Robbie?

Uncle Bob Where's the bag, sweetheart?

Madeleine Where's the bag? Where's the *bag*? I'm talking about your indiscretion, (*Takes his hand.*) I'm not talking about luggage – yes sexually he's all over the place, he's simply not continent – not that I care – it's his nature – I expect it – I encourage it – he needs the release – just you try stopping him! – isn't that right, girls? (*Approaching Hazel.*) I'll bet he's had this one already – did it hurt? – did he leave marks? – only takes him a couple of minutes – the bathroom? – or was it that sweet little bed with the heart-shaped pillow? – yes – yes – I can see it in her eyes – was it her first time, Robbie? – or can't you remember? – he never remembers, sweetheart – nothing to do with you – (*Approaching Debbie.*) And oh – oh – oh – oh – this must be the one who got pregnant – that's so sad – that is so pitiful and sad – but oh my God I suddenly realised where am I going to *change*?!

  Not in an airport toilet.
  No *way* in some shit-filled motorway service-station.
  Into a sheath like this? How?
  What d'you think, girls? Good fit?
  I can't tell you how warm and flexible it is – feels like I'm zipped into my own vagina. Pure silk. You can touch it if you like.

Mum Keep away from my children, Madeleine.

Madeleine Oh?

Mum Yes. Keep away. Keep away from my family.

Madeleine Keep away from your children? Why?

Mum Talk to her, Tom. *Say* / something.

Madeleine I thought I was a friend. I thought I was a *friend* of your children, a *friend* of your family. But okay okay   okay –

(*With new focus.*) Listen, Sandra, I realise I don't go deep. Neither of us goes deep like all of you. Do we, Robbie?

Uncle Bob I try. I have in fact been trying / here today.

Madeleine Robbie tries – but I don't even attempt it. Go deep? Why? No. And I will repeat that. No. Because this new life of ours – what will it be? Come on, Robbie – I said what will our new life be?

Uncle Bob mumbles.

What?

Uncle Bob mumbles.

What? SAY IT!

Uncle Bob Like a pane of glass.

Madeleine Thin – Tom – Sandra – girls – Terry – Peg – as a pane of glass. But of course he's told you all that. Haven't you.

Uncle Bob Yes, I've told them all that. Please – let's fetch the / bag now.

Madeleine Hard. Clear. Sharp. Clean.

And if any one of you so much as *touches* it, you'll be cut right through – right through to the bone.

They can keep the bag. Kiss, Robbie. (*Slight pause.*) I said kiss.

Uncle Bob cautiously kisses her lips. Finding she accepts this, he attempts to make the kiss deeper and more sexual. Madeleine lets this progress, then tactfully pushes him back, and looks at the others in triumph.

And music!

She sings:

> I don't need a woman to unzip my zip
> or a man with a white arse cracking the whip
> or some kind of what? fixed human relationship?

>> Some people you lose
>> Some people you keep:
>> yes I'm a family friend
>> but I don't go deep
>> (no I never go deep)

> I sit out in my car and I want to scream –
> my skin erupts – I'm rubbing in cream –
> oh why can't the world be hard, sharp and clean?

>> Yes I'm often in pain
>> there are days I weep
>> like a nymph by a stream –
>> but it doesn't go deep
>> (no it never goes deep)

> As a family friend it's my duty to say
> I'm leaving you now – yes – I'm going away –
> but if I was tempted to come back some day –

>> went into the room
>> where your kids were asleep
>> and pushed pins in their eyes –
>> then I wouldn't go deep
>> (really – trust me – I never go deep)

> But listen: I'm not some kind of inhuman thing –
> you're not to imagine I don't want to sing
> when pear-blossom garlands the pear-tree in spring

>> that I've got no soul
>> that my heart can't leap
>> when the bud unfolds –
>> just it doesn't go deep
>> (no it never goes deep)

I've booked my ticket: I'm flying first class
to a cool place thin as a pane of glass
where I just have to swipe a security pass
to swim in the milk of thick white stars.

> It's a new kind of world
> and it doesn't come cheap
> and you'll only survive
> if you don't go deep
> (so I never
> no I never
> no I never go deep)

THE FIVE ESSENTIAL FREEDOMS
OF THE INDIVIDUAL

1 THE FREEDOM TO WRITE THE SCRIPT
OF MY OWN LIFE

2 THE FREEDOM TO SEPARATE MY LEGS
(IT'S NOTHING POLITICAL)

3 THE FREEDOM TO EXPERIENCE
HORRID TRAUMA

4 THE FREEDOM TO PUT IT
ALL BEHIND ME AND MOVE ON

5 THE FREEDOM TO LOOK GOOD
& LIVE FOR EVER

I

THE FREEDOM TO WRITE THE SCRIPT
OF MY OWN LIFE

— I write the script of my own life. I make myself
what I am. This is my unique face – and this is my
unique voice. Nobody – listen – speaks the way I
do now. Nobody looks like me and nobody – I said
listen – nobody can imitate this way of speaking.

— I am the one.

— I am the one.

— I am the one – yes – writing the script.

— I am the one – yes – writing the script of my own
life now.

Pause.

I said I am the one writing the script. Nobody looks
like me. Nobody speaks the way I do now. Nobody
can imitate this way of speaking.

— No way.

— No way can anyone speak like I do. I make myself
what I am: I'm free – okay? – to invent myself as
I go along.

— Yes I invent myself as I go along. I am the one who
makes me what I am.

— I said I am the one who makes me what I am –
okay? I've got my own voice: I don't repeat what
other people say.

— No way do I repeat what other people say. I am the one who writes the script.

— Yes I am the one writing the script of my own life now. It's me who makes me what I am – not Mum, not Dad.

— No way is it Mum or Dad making me what I am. No way do I repeat what other people say or follow – obviously – any kind of script.

— Fuck that.

— Fuck – obviously following any kind of script. I am in control – fact.

— I said it is a fact I am in control of my own life – I choose how I dress – I choose how to live.

— I dress how I dress – I live exactly how I live.

— I live how I choose to live *plus* do what I do.

— I do just what I do: I don't not do it.

— Yes please don't come here telling me I don't do what I do or do do what I don't. Don't you try telling me I don't live how I live. I am strong. I have choices. I can destroy Mum's toilet brush. I can destroy Dad's tools.

— I can build a space rocket in my own back garden – yes – *plus* – if I so choose – can destroy Dad's tools: the pin-hammer and the drill.

— Yes it's me who destroys Dad's high-speed electric drill, and it's me who destroys Mum's pink toilet brush. I destroy her sofa now she's lost her mind plus the two matching chairs. I destroy their TV. I take a sledgehammer and destroy their bed and the bedside lamp and bedside clock. I destroy Mum's bedside table and her dressing table with the three mirrors. With an axe – fact – I destroy the wobbly chair. With an axe – fact – I destroy the picture of two swans. I am the one who destroys Mum's wardrobe. I am the one who destroys Dad's wardrobe now he's dead and smashes the glass ashtray. I smash the white plastic sun-lounger, I smash the garden tools – the hoe – the rake. I destroy the Saturday tea-trolley with the detachable tray. It's me who destroys the pots and pans and the electric mixer – yes the electric mixer and the cupboard contents I mean all the plates bowls knives forks spoons and packets of food like macaroni. I destroy the old toys – the doll called Sarah plus James Bond in his original James Bond car. I take Dad's hearing aid and smash it *like this*! between two bricks. It's okay: I can handle it.

— Yes.

— I write the script and I can handle it.

— Yes.

— It's up to me.

— Yes totally up to me – I write the script and I can handle it.

— Don't you come here telling me I can't. Don't you come here telling me I don't know how to live or that I'm not desirable. Fuck off if you don't like the way I speak.

— Fuck off if you don't like my religion, yes, or the way I speak.

— Just so totally fuck off if you don't like my what? what? what? – come on – say it – what? – my disability?

— Racist.

— Anti-semite.

— Body fascist.

— Cunt.

— You terrorist – you body-fascist cunt.

— Fuck off if you don't like my heels or my short skirt. Don't you come here telling me how to dress: I have a unique style.

— I have a unique style.

— I have my own – yes – quite totally unique style: the heels – the skirt – or it may be a little hat.

— I may wear a little hat or I may cover my head entirely – it's my business how I cover my head and what I cover my head with. I am the one who writes the script.

— I'm writing the script right now – I'm choosing right here right now the course of my own life right now plus I am making sense of it.

— You think my life doesn't make sense? You think I've what? I've forgotten my own password?

— You seriously think I can't open the document of my own life? –

— *Wrong!*

— – can't change what I like? – can't delete whatever I like?

— *Wrong!*

— You seriously think I can't delete my own parents or alter the way I look? You seriously think I can't make changes to my own body and save them?

— *Wrong!*

— – or tell you when to fuck me or tell you when to stop? You seriously believe I can't access my deepest love 24–7 and deepen it still more? You think I don't have those skills? –

— *Wrong!*

— – can't write my own script? – can't turn a sex crime to my advantage? – can't turn a chicken sandwich or the scream of an abducted child to my own personal advantage?

— *Wrong!*

— You think I don't know how to click on trauma and drag it into the document of my own life? You think I don't know where to insert the space rocket?

— *Wrong!*

— Yes – just so completely wrong, because I will insert the space rocket right here. I have the will. I have the voice. I have the style. I have the energy and materials. Why should I wait? See me light the twigs. Watch me ignite in my own back garden the rocket-motor of damp leaves. Soon I'll be higher than the garden swing, higher even than the roof of my own house. Yes and all those sad engineers of pure social misery who hate me to be weightless can only watch through cardboard pinholes as my own private rocket blasts towards Orion – mighty hunter! – great X in the winter sea of stars! – and moves magnificently into orbit. Let them try and control me then! – let them attempt to impose gravity! Watch me toss my piss-stained pyjamas from ten miles up into their grey faces! See me step out of my rocket wrapped in a bright suit of aluminium cooking foil, and set off, lungs glowing with pure oxygen, to track down the lost mass of the universe!

*

Acceleration smears my face
as I go deeper into space
the earth gets smaller and recedes.
But not to worry: I don't care –
I've got clean sheets and nice clean underwear:
I've everything a human being needs.

It's not as if I'll be alone:
I've got the latest touch-screen telephone
plus all the different apps and leads –
and naturally Mum made me bring
Big Teddy and the garden swing –
yes everything a human being needs.

I write the script – key in the stars –
key in long rows of storage jars
in which I keep fresh human eggs and seeds.
What's wrong? Am I perverse
to fill my private universe
with everything a human being needs?

Check the controls – it's cold out there! –
no gas, no mass, no gravity or air –
zero is what each meter reads.
But not to worry – I shan't die –
I write the script and that is why
I've got a private oxygen supply –
lungs that inflate – a heart that bleeds –
Oh yes! I've everything a human being needs.

2
THE FREEDOM TO SEPARATE MY LEGS
(IT'S NOTHING POLITICAL)

— I'm happy to separate my legs. I said I am happy to separate my legs – and when I say I'm happy to separate my legs, I mean it. I mean what I say.

— I mean what I mean.

— I mean what I say I mean: I mean I am happy to separate my legs – look.

— It's not like I'm talking in code.

— It's not one of those things where people are talking in code.

— I don't talk in code. I don't say I'm happy to separate my legs so that people who've been educated in a certain way or have particular beliefs can sit here in this audience and think that I mean the opposite – no way.

— No way do I mean the opposite.

— It's not one of those horrible things where people all mean the opposite of what they say.

— No way am I speaking in code – or trying to what? trying to represent something. I am what I am – not part of a group.

— No way am I part of a group.

— I don't join groups – I don't want trouble – I'm happy to separate my legs – look.

— I don't want to cause trouble at the airport: I raise my arms, I separate my legs, I let myself be searched. The longer I'm searched, the safer I feel. Plus I'm happy to queue: it's logical.

— I said: it's logical to queue.

— It's logical to queue, it's logical to pass through the arch of a metal-detector one at a time. It makes sense to go back if the alarm sounds, it makes sense to be searched and filmed. It's not like I'm looking for trouble.

— No I'm not looking for trouble at the airport. If the alarm sounds I separate my legs.

— I'm separating my legs. I'm letting my body be touched. It's a normal body, it doesn't represent anything. My body's okay. I've got an okay bum.

— This is my bum – it doesn't represent anything. My bum's not part of a group. My bum is happy to accept the way things are *plus* there is nothing hidden inside it.

— I've nothing hidden inside my anus. My vagina is empty. I let my vagina be searched. The deeper you reach into my vagina the safer we both feel – it's nothing political – there is nothing political about my body.

— There is nothing political about my body and there is nothing political about my holidays.

— Nothing at all.

— Nothing political at all.

— I said there's nothing political about my holidays at all – I come back refreshed – it's not like I've something to hide – I separate my legs.

— I separate my legs, I let myself be searched plus open my bag. I've nothing to hide – here are my things – holiday trousers, holiday hat. I'm not carrying an illegal cheese.

— No way am I carrying an illegal cheese or an illegal vegetable. These are my own children.

— Yes these are my own small children. I haven't stolen them, I'm not trafficking them. Their vaginas as you can see are empty and so are their cuddly toys.

— Oh sweet!

— There's nothing political about my children or my children's schools. My children as you can perfectly well see are one hundred per cent normal – raise their arms, separate their legs, produce their own documents –

— Produce – yes – their own tiny documents on demand, wait patiently while their toys are searched, and if God forbid I were to smack one round the head that poor poor child would be taken into immediate state protection. Because I admire the state. I said I admire the state. And when I say I admire the state it's not so that people who've been educated in a certain way can what? can smile sideways at their neighbour and think I believe the opposite. No: I admire the state. I admire its mechanisms for protecting my child just as I admire its systems for killing the unborn. It is proper to scan. It is proper to weed out the human material that could spoil my holiday, leaving me less refreshed.

— Oh excellent screening mechanisms! Oh scans of the whole human body!

— Scans of my holiday trousers! Oh probing radiographs of an illicit cheese!

— Deep scanning of the iris of my eye!

— Cheese scans – deep scanning of my eyes plus click to explore my bank account plus click to identify my date of birth and current regime of drugs – I've nothing to hide.

— I've nothing at all to hide: my medication's in this bag – see for yourself – it's not political.

— My medication's in a transparent bag – it's not political – the deeper I medicate the safer we both feel – the deeper I medicate myself – the deeper I medicate my child.

— The deeper I medicate my own child, the safer we both feel. I have a right to identify the molecule.

— I have a right to scan my own child. I have a human right – yes – to identify the molecule that makes my child unhappy or stops my child concentrating or that makes him scream.

— Oh look at my child run round the airport screaming!

— Oh sweet!

— If my child runs round the airport screaming, I give him the medication. If he coughs – if he fails to concentrate.

— If my child says fuck to Immigration. If my child calls an air steward you cunt.

— If my child says you cunt to a uniformed officer with a machine gun or begins to lash out with his fists, I medicate.

— Oh sweet!

— I pin my child down: I give him the pink syrup – I feed him the yellow capsule.

— He loves to be pinned down – he loves the struggle to force open his jaws – and how calm –

—   – yes how calm he is now after the pink syrup –
how intelligent after the one-hundred-milligram
capsule – *plus* he's begun to read –

—   Oh sweet! – he's beginning to read!

—   – can pick out the names of chemicals and of
chemical manufacturers – can recognise the word
drowsiness, can spell the word discolouration. He
can even pop his own capsule through the gap in
his own teeth. He can even do sums!

—   I'm so proud of the way he does his sums – knows
there are a thousand milligrams in a gram and that
a thousand grams make up a kilo. He even knows
the per-kilo cost!

—   Yes my own small child knows the per-kilo cost of
his own medication. I'm so proud.

—   I'm so proud.

—   I'm so proud of my own child.

—   Yes so proud when he tots up the per-kilo cost and
he gets it right. Plus now when I read to him from
a proper grown-up story book how he goes shiny-
eyed! How he drinks in a delicious story full of life
and full of fully imagined characters so real they can
almost be touched! Watch him absorb the funny
and human things they say. See how he follows the
slippery antics of Susan and Bill – and of Susan's
best friend Jenny. Oh how deeply Bill loves Susan –
but how little he trusts her! He locks her away –
but even when she's locked away she lies – sneaks
out – goes back to her old friend Jenny – sprawls
on the soft divan and separates her legs. And Bill
finds out. Oh yes, the agony when Bill finds out
she's wet between the legs for Jenny! But instead of
confronting her, he only makes more promises and
gives her – Susan, I mean – ever more extravagant

gifts! A dress! A luxury motor car! Oh such is
jealousy! Such the complex self-lacerating agony of
human love! – but hey hey hey – it's not that I'm a
snob about this.

— No way am I a snob.

— No way.

— No way am I saying – what? – that there's one kind
of high-brow text-based entertainment for me and
my own small gifted and intelligent child and some
other kind of entertainment – some kind of – well
let me see – hmm – what? – some kind of screen-
based proletarian trash? – really? – is that what you
think? – for the less gifted? – for the what? for the
poor? Come on. You're joking. Don't give me that
shit.

— Don't you come here giving me that shit about rich
and poor – grow up – yes you heard what I said:
grow up – this is nothing to do with politics – this
is about me and how I feel.

— This is entirely about the way I feel.

— I feel what I feel: I can't not feel it.

— How can I not feel what I feel about my own child?
How can I not feel what I feel about my own
feelings? Because it's a fact that I feel what I feel
plus whatever I feel is a fact. Is a pure fact. Don't
you come here telling me it isn't. Don't you come
here telling me I should what? should resist security.
Why should I resist security? No. I need security.
I believe in security. I complete security. I zip up my
bag.

— I snap shut – look – my vagina – I proceed to the
gate.

*

There's nothing political about my children's schools –
there's nothing political about targeting certain molecules –
or about how I choose my holidays or hospitals:
DON'T GIVE ME THAT SHIT
JUST KEEP YR NOSE OUT OF IT!

There's nothing political about stories of child-abduction –
there's nothing political about my human right to
liposuction –
to the drug that I want or to the profits of drug-production:
DON'T GIVE ME THAT SHIT
JUST KEEP YR NOSE OUT OF IT!

There's nothing political about my holiday hat –
about how much I earn or who's feeding my cat –
there's nothing political about my right to be fat:
DON'T GIVE ME THAT SHIT
JUST KEEP YR NOSE OUT OF IT!

There's nothing political about replacing my heart
or about standing in line with my legs apart –
there's no place for politics in this or in any other work
of art:
DON'T GIVE ME THAT SHIT
JUST KEEP YR NOSE OUT OF IT!

Don't give me that crap about rich and poor –
stop droning on about what constitutes a just war –
don't you come here telling me what my life's supposed
to be for –
I said get that foot of yours out of my fucking door!
YOU'RE SO FULL OF SHIT!
YES YOU'RE SO FULL OF SHIT YOU CAN
KEEP YR NOSE OUT OF IT!!!

3

THE FREEDOM TO EXPERIENCE
HORRID TRAUMA

— Protect me. Terrorise me. Then protect me again.

— Protect me. Save me. Fuck me.

— Fuck me, scan me, then fuck me again. Satisfy me one hundred per cent.

— If I'm not one hundred per cent satisfied, return my money.

— Give me back my money and apologise.

— Terrorise me and apologise. Give me a new heart.

— Replace my heart with a new one. Repair my liver.

— Replace my heart and enlarge my breasts – enlarge my lips.

— Whiten my teeth plus fatten my lips. Make love to me.

— Separate my legs – make love to me – fuck me and abduct my child – surprise me on my birthday – surprise me with a kitten.

— Surprise me with dementia on my birthday, or with a lively kitten. Make me pregnant.

— Make me pregnant on my birthday. Make me pregnant age sixty-eight or still in a little dress age nine.

— Make me a nine-year-old father – scan me – bring me in for tests.

—   Fuck and abduct my child plus bring me in for
    tests – test my blood – test my saliva – I have a
    right – swab my mouth.

—   Take blood – scan my body – make scans of my
    brain – I have a right –

—   I have a right to be scanned – I have a right to be
    offered a full range of serious diseases: terrible
    cancer, terrible suffering.

—   I have a human right to terrible suffering *plus* to a
    horrid accident.

—   Oh my horrid and entirely avoidable accident! Oh
    my worrying impotence!

—   My failure to prolong intercourse.

—   My failure to reach orgasm.

—   My terrible fear of dementia – of childbirth – bad
    headaches – bad hangover – my reaction to shellfish
    – my anaphylactic shock.

—   My shock – my reaction to fresh crab.

—   My failing eyesight and stink of dental caries – my
    addiction to prescription drugs.

—   My burning urethra, my chronic weight loss, my
    diminished responsibility, my stretch-marks, my
    broken nose and sex-addiction.

—   My burning urethra, my chronic weight loss, my
    diminished responsibility, stretch-marks, broken
    nose and sex-addiction *plus* my addiction to
    morphine *plus* my addiction to shopping.

—   My burning urethra, my chronic weight-loss,
    diminished responsibility, stretch-marks, broken
    nose and sex-addiction, addiction to morphine,

addiction to shopping *plus* my post-traumatic stress *plus* my infertility *plus* my long long history of abuse.

— My trauma! My horrid abuse!

— My years of horrid abuse at the hands of those I trusted: my abusive mother, my abusive priest.

— My abusive father. My manipulative and abusive cat.

— My horrid abusive baby plus flashbacks of my abusive priest. Take blood.

— Take blood – scan my whole body – authenticate my abuse.

— Swab my mouth – authenticate my horrid trauma – offer me therapy.

— Offer me therapy – save me.

— Save me.

— Test me.

— Offer me counselling.

        — Authenticate me – fuck me.

        (*Softly.*) I said fuck me . . . go on [= *continue*] . . . go on . . .

— Offer me a full range of anxieties.

— Protect me.

        stop.

— Abduct me.

        I said fuck me . . .

— Surprise me with therapy on my birthday. Fatten my lips.

        go on . . . stop.

— Traumatise me with a lively kitten. Whiten my brown teeth.

        I said fuck me . . . fuck me . . . go on . . .

—   Remove and replace   go on . . .
     my heart.
                              yes go on . . .

                              go on . . .

                              . . .

                              . . .

                              stop.

4
THE FREEDOM TO PUT IT
ALL BEHIND ME AND MOVE ON

— Yes I decided I needed therapy. I decided I needed to change. There were things about my past I wasn't confronting. I needed to confront them and move on.

— For example –

— For example – yes – I'd never talked to anyone about my Mum. I'd never talked to anyone about my Mum and Dad. I'd never talked to anyone about my childhood.

— I had flashbacks –

— Yes I had flashbacks of my childhood plus I had problems with my sexual partner.

— I had problems I was not confronting: intimacy, for example – trust.

— I had problems with trust, I had problems with my body, I had problems with my partner's body. There were things about my body I wasn't confronting.

— I was angry.

— I was angry. I needed to put my anger behind me and move on.

— Yes I was angry about my partner's body. I couldn't talk. I couldn't talk to my partner about my anger. I couldn't talk to my partner about my Mum and Dad. I couldn't talk about the flashbacks. I needed to put my flashbacks behind me and move on.

— I needed to talk to Dad. But how could I talk to Dad? I'd never talked to Dad. Dad never talked to me.

— Dad never talked to me and Dad never talked to Mum. Dad never talked. Did Dad have flashbacks? If Dad had flashbacks he never talked about them and if the phone rang Dad never answered it.

— Dad never answered the phone. The phone rang on and on, Dad never answered it. Were there problems Dad wasn't confronting? Things about his body? – things about the telephone? Did Dad have flashbacks? I couldn't talk to him.

— I could not talk to Dad. I could not talk to anyone *about* my dad. I could not talk to anyone about my mother's sister. I tried.

— I tried.

— I tried.

— I tried to talk about my mother's sister with my partner but there were problems: there were problems with my partner's body and there were problems with my partner's cat. I was angry.

— I was angry with my partner's cat. I was angry with my partner's body. I had flashbacks.

— I had flashbacks where I saw snow – could see snow – could see a garden under snow – black stalks of the currant bush – snow squeezed into my woollen mitten – there's Dad by the space rocket burning the pile of leaves, look – then it's gone.

— Snow falling from a grey sky into my face, look – then it's gone.

—   There's the smell of the damp mitten, there's Mum
    wheeling in the tea-trolley with the Saturday tea,
    look – then it's gone. There's that hard tapping on
    the glass – there, there, listen! – then it's gone.
    What did the flashbacks mean?

—   What did the flashbacks mean? Why was I angry
    with my partner's cat? Why when my partner
    touched me did I flinch away? Was it the cat?

—   Was it the cat or was it my mother's sister? Why
    was my mother's sister tapping at the window?
    Why did it make that sound? What was she tapping
    with – was it a key? I'd stopped enjoying food.

—   I'd stopped enjoying food and I'd stopped enjoying
    sex. I'd stopped enjoying moderate violence.

—   I'd stopped enjoying mushrooms. I needed to move
    on. I needed to change.

—   Yes.

—   I needed to think positively about my body.

—   Yes.

—   I needed to think positively about my sexual partner.

—   Yes.

—   And about my job.

—   I hated my job.

—   I really hated my job. Sorry. It's true. I hated it. I
    hated my boss. I hated her quiet way of standing
    behind me when I worked. The way she ate
    sandwiches angered me.

—   The way she poked at the filling.

—   The way she poked at the filling with her fingernail, the way she said Hmm not much chicken.

—   The way my boss said Not much chicken angered me: I couldn't talk to her. I tried.

—   I tried.

—   I tried.

—   I tried and tried to talk to her about my job, I tried to talk to her about my Dad, about my flashbacks. I tried and tried to talk to her about enjoying sex but there was trauma: there was trauma in my boss's past. Why else would she poke a sandwich? Why else would she paint her fingernails bright green? My boss was damaged. Maybe her parents – who knows what? Was it about race? Was it about class? I refused to speculate.

—   Was it about my boss's sexuality? I refused to speculate.

—   Was it about the strip of light under her parents' bedroom door? Or under her own door? Or under some other door – the bathroom door? Was it about alcohol?

—   Was it about misuse of alcohol or of prescription drugs? Was there a long long history for example of mental illness? I refused to speculate.

—   I totally refused to speculate about my boss. I hated her, I couldn't talk to her, I couldn't talk to her about my job. I was trapped.

—   I was trapped. I was boxed-in. I was hurt. I was fearful. I was angry. I was ashamed.

—   I was hurt. I was silent. I was closed off. I was ugly.

329

—   I was guilty. I was trapped.

—   I was boxed in by my boss.

—   I was ugly, I was fat.

—   I was fat, I was too thin, I was too hurt.

—   I was blocked, I was trapped, I was too ashamed.

—   I was angry.

—   I was angry.

—   I was angry now my Dad was dead. How could I talk to Dad now Dad was dead? How could I talk to Dad about my flashbacks? Now I would never talk to Dad about my boss's chicken or my mother's sister's tapping. Now I would never talk to Dad about Dad's body. Dad was dead.

—   My Dad was dead and I would never talk to him.

—   I would never talk to Dad about my Mum. I would never talk to Dad about the lost mass of the universe. I was alone. Yes I was alone. I hated my feet.

—   I hated – that's right – to see my own feet. I hated – yes this is right – to see between my own legs now Dad was dead. I flinched from my partner, flinched from my partner's gaze. There were things about my body I could not confront. I needed to put these things behind me and move on. I wore socks.

—   I wore socks. I covered my feet. I at all times covered my feet and covered between my legs. I was fearful, I was boxed-in by my partner's gaze. I could not love, I could not love myself or trust my partner. I could not separate my legs or trust my partner with my love. I could not eat meat. I could

330

not eat sugar. I could not eat mushrooms. I could
not eat wheat or dairy products. I could not look
confidently between my partner's legs. I could not
lie confidently across my partner's stomach.

— I could not eat nuts: there was no nut I could eat.
I sicked up nuts.

— I sicked up meat. I sicked up fish now Dad was
dead. I sicked up cheese. I sicked up marzipan.

— I picked through my own sick. I picked through my
own sick while my sexual partner was asleep and
ate it.

— I ate my own sick then sicked my sick up again
over my socks. My socks were pink. My socks were
dark blue. I wore thick orange socks. I couldn't
sleep.

— I wore thick orange socks. I tried to watch sex.

— I wore thick orange socks. I tried to watch moderate
sex. I tried to watch strong sex and frequent bloody
violence. I couldn't sleep. I crawled into bed.

— I crawled into my bed and covered between my
legs. I covered my head. My socks were pink. I
couldn't sleep.

— I could taste sick. My partner slept. I could not
trust my partner with my love. The room was
dark. I covered my head. I covered between my
legs. I saw Dad's currant bushes crowned with
snow.

Long silence.

*

331

Oh help me – please – I need to confess:
I'm addicted to chocolate – shopping – I'm
    scared of sex –
trapped, hurt, angry – plus there's the stress of those
                PANIC ATTACKS!
Hey   hey   hey – be calm – relax –
Just sing my little therapeutic song
then put it all behind you and move on.

Oh help me – please – I need to explain:
the abusive priest – the strip of light – the pain –
bitterness in my mouth – the wet piss stain and the
                HORRID FLASHBACKS!
Hey   hey   hey – be calm – relax –
Just sing my little therapeutic song
then put it all behind you and move on.

Oh please please – help! – they say it's me
used my own child for child pornography
and that in point of fact it was my own family
                I KILLED WITH AN AXE!!
Hey   hey   hey – calm down – relax –
Just sing my little therapeutic song
then put it all behind you and move on.

Oh help me – listen to me – please – please –
turns out I rounded up these Palestinian refugees –
shot all the young men against a wall
then the next day couldn't remember anything
    about it at all!
Not only that but when I clicked on the news
they were saying I'd massacred over six million
    Jews!
burned whole forests! – broke faith! – spat at
    the poor! –
trashed the planet! – started an endless illegal war
            PLUS I AVOIDED TAX!!!

Hey   hey   hey   hey – come on – calm down –
   relax –
Just sing my little therapeutic song –
we don't use words here like right and wrong –
say to yourself I deserve love I am strong –
then put it all behind you
     put it all behind you
just put it all behind you and move on.

5

THE FREEDOM TO LOOK GOOD
& LIVE FOR EVER

— I've moved on. I'm looking good. I look in the mirror: I like what I see.

— I'm looking good. I eat.

— I eat chocolate. I eat ice cream. I exercise. I look in the mirror: not bad!

— I eat a vegetable. It's a good vegetable. I eat a piece of meat.

— I eat meat, I eat a vegetable, I exercise, I look in the mirror, I like what I see.

— I eat, I look, I check.

— I check my weight.

— I check my look.

— I check my chocolate: yes my chocolate's still there.

— I check my vegetable, I'm checking my meat.

— I check my blood, I check my lung.

— I check for lumps.

— I eat, I look, I check my look, I meet my own eyes, I'm looking good.

— I'm checking for lumps: no lumps.

— I eat a fruit. I eat a chocolate. Oh yummy!

— I'm looking good. I'm looking pretty good. I said
I'm looking pretty good – look at me.

— Yes.

— Look at me.

— Yes.

— Look at me.

— Yes.

— I'm looking pretty good. I'm looking pretty
desirable. I'm working out. I look like a good fuck.

— I look like a good fuck. I look like I've got friends.

— I've got good friends. I'm checking my friends.

— I'm fucking my good friends then checking my
weight. I eat fish.

— I eat fish. I eat fruit. I'm checking between my legs –
checking my balls for lumps. I'm checking my hair
for hair-loss plus checking my heart.

— I'm checking my skin for tell-tale signs. I'm checking
my heart for lumps. I exercise: I can swim, I can
run, I can stand on one leg.

— I can stand really well on one leg – fact.

— It's a fact I can eat fruit. It's a fact I can stand on
one leg. Oh look at the fine fruit spray as I break
the peel.

— Look at the fine spray: smell this fine orange. Look
at me. I said look at me. Look at me eat fruit.
Look at my mouth – not just the teeth – look past
the teeth, look right past my tongue – look into my
throat – come right into my throat and enter my
stomach – enter my stomach, pass into my gut –

look round, yes, take a good look round my gut, check it out, check out my nice long gut and emerge from my arse. Look at me. Look at my arse.

— I check my weight. I check my arse. Look at my arse. It's a pretty good arse!

— I'm bicycling.

— I'm bicycling a *lot*!

— I like to use my bike a *lot*! I check the distance travelled. I check the time taken. I'm getting so fast and fit! As each day goes by I shave off another second and reward myself with a chocolate. I envy you. I wish I could see my own arse from behind the way you can see my arse from behind when you're behind me. I wish I could see myself swim.

— I wish I could watch myself actually live – yes just see myself being alive and continuing to be alive and being perpetually alive and going on and on and on like this living – not like in previous times when people – remember? – stopped living and died *plus* there was so much shit.

— Yes there was so much shit, wasn't there, in previous times.

— There was so much shit about how badly things were going – yawn yawn – about how people stopped living and died. I mean I'd had it up to here with how little fish there was – or how little cash – with how children sickened, with how it was all so bad and fucking difficult and yawn yawn yawn – I just wanted to rock back in my chair and scream.

— Everybody had bad haircuts.

— Everybody had really bad haircuts *plus* they were being rounded up and shot *or* their children sickened *or* there was an imminent I don't know what –

— Catastrophe.

— Catastrophe. A wave.

— Some catastrophic wave.

— Yes there was a wave or a dearth. There could be a blaze.

— The world was always ending, that's right, in a blaze of light or there could be a dearth. Time passed – oh yes – but time made nothing better – time made you feel like shit.

— Time made you feel like you'd wasted your life: either spent your life with the wrong person or never found the right person to spend it with – remember? – *or* spent your whole life with the right person but never of course realised until that person sickened and died and you were alone yes utterly alone and yawn yawn yawn – *then* came the wave, then came the whatever the annihilating blaze of light. There was so much complete shit, so much horrid emptiness: nobody swam, nobody biked, nobody ate fruit. I'd go into a shoe shop and there would be no shoes, or go into a theatre and there would be whatever –

— There would be no play.

— No play – whatever – what kind of fucking world was that?

— Yes I'd go into a food shop in previous times and find there would be no food, or into a bank and the

bank would be out of cash. I just wanted to rock
back in my chair and scream and scream. But *now* –

—   But *now* –

—   But *now* –

—   But *now* –

—   Yes but *now* –

—   Because *now* –

—   Yes but *now* –

—   Yes *now* –

—   Because what I am saying is that now when I go
into the fish shop there's fish – there is fish – mullet
and the red snapper – fresh crab.

—   There is – yes – mullet in the fish shop and ripe
plums at the fruiterer's *plus* if I want those rope-
soled boating loafers in the shoe shop then I'll buy
them. I will buy the loafers. I will boat in them.

—   I will boat – fact – in the rope-soled loafers – bob
on the ocean – dive from the varnished deck.

—   I jump from the deck – fact. Dive – swim – smash
up spray.

—   I smash up spray.

—   I like to smash up spray a *lot*! Look how I bob –
look how I float in the hot white light.

—   I float in the hot white sunlight near the boat a *lot*!
Then climb a rope. Then sip on a cold drink, bite
on a hot snack.

—   I climb on my hot friend on the boat. I bite on my
friend's lip. I'm snacking on fresh fish.

— I'm snacking on fish. I'm fucking my good friend.

— I'm biting. I'm biting my friend's mouth now. I sip on my friend's blood. I'm wetting my lips with blood plus snacking on fresh crab.

— I'm snacking on fresh crab a *lot*! I'm biting a *lot*! I'm biting down hard. I'm snacking on blood a *lot*! Look at my wet lips. Look at my stiff cock.

— I said my wet lips. I said my stiff cock.

— I said bright eyes, smooth skin. I said my slippery vagina.

— I said thick hair.

— I said flat belly and good fuck.

— I said my bike.

— I said I will live for ever – look at me.

— Yes.

— Look at me.

— Yes.

— I said I will live for ever – *look at me*.

Pause.

You're looking?

— Yes.

— Because my personal wealth and own privately acquired horizons are growing day by day – and day by day I am becoming more and more reasonable and more – yes you heard what I said – more so totally understanding of my own enormous capabilities that I can feel – yes can feel the time

coming when thanks to the indefinite extension of
my life I will be in a position to realise the potential
not just of my boat, not just of my bike and arse
and smiling eyes – not just of my sharp teeth – but
of the whole expanding spinning constellation of
my intelligence – don't you see? I said to you: don't
you see?

Pause.

I check my vegetable. I'm checking my blood for
lumps. I'm looking good.

*

My body's toned and you've probably seen
me running right past on my running machine
and my brain is alert and my bloodstream's clean –

> You won't see me die –
> it's not that kind of show –
> I cling on to life
> and I don't let go
> (no I never let go)

I'll always look good and I'll always have fun
plus I'll always have sex and repeatedly come
and I'll look in the mirror and always be young –

> With my sharp white teeth
> in a long clean row
> I bite into life
> and I don't let go
> (no I never let go)

I'm checking my chocolate – yes my chocolate's
    still there
plus I've got this new way now of doing my hair
so it kind've sticks up – look, like this – in the air –

which is kind've unique –
yes I think you should know
I've a right to life
and I'm not letting go
(no I never let go)

Yes I'm looking good – there's my hair – there's
   my eyes –
there's my firm round calves and scissoring thighs –
my expanding brain – it's incredible (just take
   a look at it) size –

plus a mouth full of crab –
but even so
I bite down hard
and I don't let go
(no I never let go)

Yes I'll always look good and I'll always be fun
and use my machine to run run run –
I'll have strong frequent sex and I'll violently come
till my blood streams hot and my mind turns
   numb –

Yes I'll set my teeth
in a long clean row
bite down hard
and never let go

(no I'll never
no I'll never
no I'll never let go)

IN THE REPUBLIC OF HAPPINESS

Tu non se' in terra, sì come tu credi
Paradiso, I, 91

*An enormous room. Daylight. Large windows suggest
a green landscape – but the landscape is indistinct.*
*The room is completely empty – except, perhaps, for
what looks like an abandoned office-type desk.*
Uncle Bob is alone. He listens.

Uncle Bob Maddy?
  Maddy?
  Madeleine?

He listens.

Maddy?

*Madeleine enters in the haute couture dress. She
smiles.*

Madeleine What?

Uncle Bob Where were you?

Madeleine I was having a sandwich.

Uncle Bob Was it nice?

Madeleine Yes. It was chicken. I enjoyed it.

Uncle Bob Where did you find it?

Madeleine Find it? I made it. I made it with chicken.

Uncle Bob Oh?

Madeleine Yes.

Uncle Bob Where did you find the chicken?

Madeleine Where did I find the chicken? Well it was in the sandwich. It was delicious. I enjoyed it. Would you like one?

Uncle Bob Would I . . .?

Madeleine Yes – like a sandwich.

Uncle Bob No.

Madeleine Are you sure?

Uncle Bob No.

Madeleine Not with chicken?

Uncle Bob No. Thank you.

    Pause.

Madeleine So?

Uncle Bob So?

Madeleine Are you ready?

Uncle Bob Am I ready for what?

Madeleine How many times do I have to ask you?

Uncle Bob Have to ask me what?

Madeleine Robbie?

Uncle Bob What? Have to ask me what?

    Pause.

Madeleine Is something the matter?

Uncle Bob Is it?

Madeleine No – I'm asking you.

Uncle Bob You're asking me what?

Madeleine You – you – is something the matter with you?

Uncle Bob (*with humour*) Like what? No. Bitch. Of course not.

Madeleine (*laughing*) Bitch?

Uncle Bob Mmm?

Madeleine (*laughing*) Did you just call me a bitch, Robbie?

Uncle Bob When?

Madeleine In this conversation.

Uncle Bob I can't remember.

Madeleine But you just said it.

Pause. He stares at her.

What is it you're staring at? Have I got crumbs?

Uncle Bob Mmm?

Madeleine Have I got crumbs round my mouth? Am I all smeared with chicken? Do I look sweet? I said: do I look sweet, Robbie?

She wipes her mouth with her fingers.

Well? What is it?

Uncle Bob (*smiling*) I have so much to remember.

Madeleine No you don't. What d'you mean? Remember what?

Uncle Bob The things you've said I'm to say.

Madeleine I haven't said to say anything.

Uncle Bob No. [*Not true.*]

Madeleine I haven't said you're to say anything: you can say what you like.

Uncle Bob No.

Madeleine Yes you can, Robbie – you know you can – whatever you like. You can call me bitch, you can say I look sweet, you can say just whatever you like. Go on. Say it.

What's wrong?

Uncle Bob (*lowers his eyes*) Help me.

Madeleine Is that what you're saying?

Uncle Bob Help me.

Madeleine Is that what you're actually saying or do you mean help you to say something else?

Uncle Bob What?

Madeleine I said: is 'help me' what you're actually saying or do / you mean –?

Uncle Bob I don't know. You said I could say anything.

Madeleine Provided it makes sense – it has to make sense, Robbie – don't you see how important that is? There have to be rules.

Uncle Bob Whose rules?

Madeleine Well my rules, of course – don't you see how important that is?

Pause. He reflects.

What?

Uncle Bob Don't leave me, Madeleine.

Madeleine (*faint laugh*) Leave you? Why would I leave you?

Uncle Bob I know you.

Madeleine Oh?

Uncle Bob Yes I know what you're like.

Madeleine What am I like, Robbie?
I said what am I like?

Uncle Bob mumbles.

What?

Uncle Bob mumbles.

What did you say? Speak up.

Uncle Bob I said: I cannot remember what you're like.

Madeleine But I'm here, Robbie. I'm right here in front of you. You can *see* what I'm like. I'm like this.

Uncle Bob No.

Madeleine Yes I am, Robbie. Look at me. I said don't turn away like that *look at me.*

He looks.

Now. Tell me what I'm like – don't say you can't remember.

Uncle Bob Ah – ah – how beautiful you are.

Madeleine Beautiful – yes – and? Come on.

Uncle Bob Cruel? Are you cruel?

Madeleine Yes of course I'm cruel – but in what way?

Uncle Bob Mmm?

Madeleine In what way – Robbie – am I cruel? Is it I kill or is it I don't fuck?

Uncle Bob Mmm?

Madeleine I said is it I kill or is it I don't fuck?

Uncle Bob I don't know.

Madeleine Or both? Is it both? Tell me.

Uncle Bob I don't know. Kill who?

Madeleine Or is it my mind?

Uncle Bob Is it?

Madeleine Tell me about my mind – come on.

Uncle Bob I can't.

Madeleine Tell me.

Uncle Bob I don't know. Is it blank?

Madeleine Blank?

Uncle Bob Yes – empty – blank.

Madeleine Is my mind empty? Is that what you think?

Uncle Bob I don't know what to say to you!

Madeleine Her mind is blank – is that what you tell our citizens?

Uncle Bob What citizens?

Madeleine In your lectures – I'm talking about the lectures you give to our citizens, Robbie – I'm talking about your job – I'm talking about / the song.

Uncle Bob But why won't you let me sleep?

Madeleine I'm sorry?

Uncle Bob Why won't you let me sleep? – Why 're you always shaking me awake?

Madeleine Well I just want to see if you're happy.

Uncle Bob But you *know* how happy I am. You don't need to shake me awake.

Madeleine Oh?

Uncle Bob You don't need to bite me.

Madeleine I bite you to wake you up. I want you to see the tree. I want you to see the white flowers. And oh – oh – Robbie – the clean spring air! – and each blade of grass like a green razor! I need you to wake up for me and smile.

Uncle Bob Don't I smile in my sleep?

Madeleine No – never – you thrash – you grind your teeth – you thrash and you reach for between my legs.

Uncle Bob That's not true.

Madeleine Yes you reach for between my legs like you're not happy. Because have you forgotten?

Uncle Bob Forgotten what? I don't know.

Madeleine You see this is what frightens me.

Uncle Bob Forgotten what, Madeleine?

Madeleine I think you've forgotten how happy you really are. I think you're starting to forget how happy this world really makes you – grinding your teeth – grabbing – thrashing. Because what do you want? What have you not got?

Pause. Uncle Bob struggles to think.

Uncle Bob Listen, sweetheart –

Madeleine Oh?

Uncle Bob Yes listen to what I am going to say.

Madeleine Oh?

Uncle Bob Yes.

Madeleine And what are you going to say?

Uncle Bob Yes.

Madeleine I said what are you going to say?

Uncle Bob What?

Madeleine I said to you what are you / going to say?

Uncle Bob I don't know – I don't know till I've said it –
but listen – listen – you   you   you say to me
'the tree' – but I don't see it – plus you say to me 'oh the
white blossom' – but where – yes – where is the branch
that carries it? And when you say to me – say to me –
'clean spring air' why don't I feel it moving across my
face? Why do I only feel your hand? Or your sharp teeth.

What lectures? Where are the citizens? Why aren't
they thronging the staircase? Or using small plastic cups
to drink coffee? Why can't I hear the small plastic cups
crackle? Is it I'm going deaf?

You talk about the world but I listen and listen and I
still can't hear it. Where has the world gone? What is it
we've done? – did we select it and click? – mmm? Have
we deleted it by mistake? Because I look out of that
window and I don't know what I'm seeing just like I'm
opening my mouth now, sweetheart – look at it – look –
opening it now – here – my mouth – now – look at it –
and I don't know what's coming out – is this what I'm
saying or is this what you've said I'm to say? How do
I know? When will I ever remember? And of course
I'm happy but I feel like I'm one of those characters
Madeleine crossing a bridge and the bridge is collapsing
behind me slat by slat by slat but I'm still running on –
why? What's holding me up?

Madeleine Robbie?

Uncle Bob (*inward*) But it's deeper than that, it's deeper
than that, the whole thing goes much / deeper than that.

Madeleine Robbie?

Uncle Bob What?

Madeleine Pay attention.

Uncle Bob Pay attention to what?

Madeleine Please don't shout. Why is it you always get like this?

Uncle Bob I always get like this.

Madeleine Yes but why do you always get like this? What're our citizens going to think – mmm? Because you need to command their respect.

Uncle Bob I do command their respect.

Madeleine Because when you're standing in front of them and those hundreds of faces are lifted towards you and those hundreds and hundreds of gleaming eyes are locked – and they will be, Robbie – locked on to yours, and those – what? – what? – must be billions – must be so many billions of malleable human cells are being moulded, Robbie – yes moulded by me through you inside each skull by the sound of each thrilling syllable of our hundred-per-cent happy song – then you need to command their respect. I said: then you need to command their respect.

Uncle Bob I do command their respect, Madeleine.

Madeleine Then say it.

Uncle Bob I do command their respect.

Madeleine With each thrilling syllable.

Uncle Bob Yes. What?

Madeleine With each thrilling / syllable.

Uncle Bob With each thrilling syllable of our song.

353

Pause.

Madeleine (*smiles*) I can take you.

Uncle Bob Where?

Madeleine I can take you to see the tree.

Uncle Bob Yes?

Madeleine What would you like me to show you? the tree? or what? something else? shall I show you the stream? or what? the stars? or what?

Uncle Bob I do command their respect.

Madeleine Yes but I'm talking about something else now – about taking a trip.

Uncle Bob Yes.

Madeleine Am I not?

Uncle Bob Yes – to the stream.

Madeleine To the stream – to the tree – we could drive.

Uncle Bob We could go in a boat.

Madeleine We could drive – we could go in a nice boat.

Uncle Bob Could we fly?

Madeleine We can do whatever we like.

Uncle Bob We could go in a boat.

Madeleine If you like.

Uncle Bob We could go in a boat.

Madeleine Yes – if you like.

Uncle Bob We could go in a nice boat.

Madeleine Yes of course we could go in a nice boat but

we'd need to smarten you up a bit first, wouldn't we.
(*Smiles.*) Look at you.

Uncle Bob Oh?

Madeleine Yes: look at you.

*She goes over to him and affectionately adjusts his
clothes. It's the first time they've been physically close.*

Why d'you always dress like this?

Uncle Bob I always dress like this.

Madeleine Yes but why?
And your eyes.

Uncle Bob And my eyes what?

Madeleine In the night.
When you shut them.
When you breathe.
When you thrash.
When you grab like that with your hand.
When I bite.
When I'm touching your face.
Don't you like me touching your face?
Kiss, Robbie.

Uncle Bob What?

Madeleine I said kiss.

Very cautiously, he kisses her lips.
*She smiles and is about to turn away when he grips
her and kisses her much harder. She struggles to get
free – a long and intense silent struggle – until he
finally gets pushed away.*

No, Robbie – *stop* – what is wrong with you?

Pause. They recover their breath.

355

Uncle Bob Don't leave me, Madeleine.

Madeleine Why would I leave you?

Uncle Bob I know you. I know what you're like.

Madeleine Then you know I won't leave you.

Pause. She walks out.

Uncle Bob Maddy?
Madeleine?

He listens.

Madeleine?
(*Inward.*) But it's deeper than that, it's deeper than
that, it goes much deeper than that.

*Strange music becomes audible – a bright repetitive
phrase – half music, half machine.
He listens.*

Madeleine?

*Madeleine reappears with the source of the sound –
a small glittering box, which she places on the floor.
She hands Uncle Bob a microphone.*

Madeleine So. Are you ready?

He nods, and begins to mumble something.

Into the microphone.

Uncle Bob What?

Madeleine Into the microphone.

*Pause. The music continues.
Uncle Bob speaks haltingly into the microphone.*

Uncle Bob Here's our 100% happy song
it's got a few words

but it doesn't last long.

Hum   hum   hum
hum the happy song.

Pause. The music continues.

We make up the words as we go along
each word is right
nothing we sing is wrong.

Hum   hum   hum
hum the happy song.

Longer pause. The music continues.

Madeleine (*sotto voce*) We smile.

Uncle Bob What?

Madeleine (*sotto voce*) We smile when / it's white.

Uncle Bob
We smile when it's white, we smile
        when the pear-tree's green –
we're the happiest that human beings
have ever so far been.

Hum   hum   hum
hum the happy song.

Pause. The music continues.

The earth – plus Mum and Dad –
        the bedside lamp – the state –
have . . . have . . .

Madeleine (*sotto voce*) have burned to ash.

Uncle Bob
have burned to ash –
yes everything's just great.

Hum   hum   hum
hum the happy song.

Long pause.

*The music suddenly stops dead and all goes dark
apart from Uncle Bob's face.*

Madeleine (*sotto voce, from the dark*) Click on my
smiling face.

Uncle Bob What?

Madeleine Click – click on my / smiling face.

Uncle Bob
Click on my smiling face and you can install
a version of this song
that has no words at all.

Madeleine Yes hum –

Uncle Bob
Yes hum   hum   hum –

Madeleine Oh hum hum hum hum hum –

Uncle Bob
Oh hum hum hum
the happy song.